DRYDEN'S POLITICAL POETRY

DRYDEN'S POLITICAL POETRY

THE TYPOLOGY OF KING AND NATION

STEVEN N. ZWICKER

Brown University Press Providence

Brown University Press, Providence, Rhode Island 02912
© 1972 by Brown University. All rights reserved
Published 1972

Chapter 3 appeared in substantially the same form in
Philological Quarterly, vol. 50, no. 4 (October 1971),
pp. 582–98, © 1971 by The University of Iowa

Set in Linotype Baskerville by Dix Typesetting Co. Inc.
Printed in the United States of America
By Connecticut Printers, Inc.
On Warren's Olde Style White Wove
Bound by Complete Books Co.
Designed by Richard Hendel

Library of Congress Cataloging in Publication Data

Zwicker, Steven N
Dryden's political poetry.

Includes bibliographical references.
1. Dryden, John, 1631–1700.   2. Politics in
literature.   3. Bible in literature.   I. Title.
PR3427.P6Z9   821'.4   70–188832
ISBN 0–87057–134–6

To Judith

CONTENTS

PREFACE

Dryden's political poetry has excited admiration and controversy from the seventeenth century to our own time. For his contemporaries, to judge by their often virulent response, Dryden's handling of topical and partisan issues must have generated much of the poetry's immediate interest. For the twentieth-century reader this can hardly be the case. The venality of a man like Slingsby Bethel or even the political ambitions of Anthony Ashley Cooper are now the province of social and political history; the attraction of Dryden's political poetry, like that of the political verse of all past ages, lies in the poet's ability to transform the objects of his contempt and admiration through the language and strategies of his art. The portraits executed by Rubens or Bronzino are interesting not primarily for what they reveal of the personalities of their subjects, nor for what they might indicate of the private convictions of the artist, but rather for the demonstrations they offer of the artist transforming his subject through the richly iconographical language of Renaissance portraiture. So with Dryden, the poet's conservative politics or the occasions of the individual poems are of less interest than the poetics of Dryden's art. Such events as the coronation of Charles II, the Exclusion Crisis, and the release of Shaftesbury from imprisonment on charges of high treason retain an interest as occasions of Dryden's poetry; but it is as literary, rather than historical, artifacts that the poems invite admiration.

Central to Dryden's methods and art as political poet is a sustained sense of history. From his first published work, the verses on the death of Lord Hastings (1649), to *The Secular Masque* (1700), Dryden displays a continuous impulse to see in the figures and events of past ages models with which he might praise, evaluate, and parallel his own time. Dryden was hardly alone in his response to the cultural and historical past. The Tudor arts of historiography and translation from the classics were perfected during the seventeeth century in works such as Clarendon's *History of the Rebellion,* Chapman's Homer, and Dryden's own translations of Virgil. Yet Dryden shared with his contemporaries more than a general sense of the importance of the past to the present day; he understood, as they did, the special meaning that sacred history had for the seventeenth century. Not only had Dryden, together with Milton and Marvell, lived through times during which Scripture was carefully examined for exact predictions of the date and character of the millennium, but he also shared with poets of the earlier seventeenth century an understanding of the importance of the language of Scripture to the interior life of the reader.

Donne had catechized himself and his audience by meditating on the relationship between Adam, Christ, and everyman; Milton, through the voice of Michael in *Paradise Lost,* taught and consoled his fallen readers by demonstrating the pattern and meaning of providential history; and Dryden turned to the political themes and occasions of the later seventeenth century with a vocabulary and from a perspective that illuminated the relationship between the present day, the sacred past, and the prophetic future. An understanding of the seventeenth-century context of Dryden's political poetry is extremely important in gauging the meaning that sacred narrative had for the poet and his audience and in appreciating the ways in which Dryden extended the particular occasions of his political poems to include the political life of his audience and the public life of all men.

Dryden's career as political poet can be read as a series of attempts to forge a sacred history for the English nation. In his Restoration panegyrics Dryden sets the particular events —the return and restoration of the king—against restorative moments in the record of redemptive history—the Old and the New Testament. Figures such as Noah and David, commonly read during the seventeenth century as prefigurations of Christ the Redeemer, are analogues for the king; and Dryden so shaped these poems that both the historical and figural meaning of the biblical characters might illuminate the role that the king plays in the life of the nation. In *Annus Mirabilis* Dryden again uses the technique of biblical allusion to suggest the meaning that figures and events of the present day drew from biblical analogues. The Dutch Naval War, the Great Fire of London, the king's redemptive prayer, and the poet's prophetic vision are seen in terms of analogous events and experiences in scriptural history. The present gains coherence and significance from its association with the record of God's chosen people in the Old Testament.

In *Absalom and Achitophel* Dryden turns from allusion and suggestion to the full terms of metaphoric history. The poem engages past and present in both a historical and figural relationship that allows Dryden to explore the fallen as well as blessed character of England's sacred history, the promise and the tensions of political life in his Anglo-Judaic Israel. The admiration that readers feel for the poem is in large part a response to the imaginative energy with which Dryden extends the terms of the poem's central metaphor while retaining the sharpness and point of the best topical verse.

The Medall, like *Absalom and Achitophel*, succeeds in satirically anatomizing the folly and wickedness of the court's opponents; as political poetry, however, it shows more openly the seams of a metaphoric fabric that could not, given the political realities of the 1680s, continue to enfold both the divinity of the Stuart monarchs and the blessed condition of the nation. And in reading from *The Medall* through *Britannia Rediviva*, one increasingly senses Dryden's difficulties with his role as political poet and with the metaphor of sacred history as a way of coming to terms with the full range of English political life. Dryden's language in the last of the political poems stiffens; he separates the king from the nation in his use of sacred metaphor; and a concurrent loss of the poet's faith in politics as a redemptive instrument can be felt.

The political poetry read as a whole suggests, then, both an approach to the individual pieces and a way of understanding Dryden's career as public poet. The possibility of considering the poems cross-referentially and in the light of a metaphoric technique that they share is obvious, but it is a task heretofore unaccomplished in Dryden criticism. Arthur Hoffman and Earl Miner have written illuminating studies of imagery and metaphor in Dryden's poetry; Bernard Schilling has provided a full discussion of the "conservative myth" in *Absalom and Achitophel;* and the editors of the California *Dryden* have scrupulously placed a number of the political poems in their historical settings. The purpose of this book is to offer an interpretation of the political poems from a different perspective, one informed by the weight of the whole on the particular and by what I take to be the importance of Renaissance traditions of typological interpretation of the Old Testament to Dryden's use of sacred metaphor. Starting with the problem of reading the language of Dryden's political poetry, specifically his scriptural metaphors, one is led to investigate, first, why the complex of biblical motifs and metaphoric identifications continued to engage a poet intent on joining in some way the roles of panegyrist, satirist, and prophet; and second, how Dryden's use of sacred history developed over the more than two decades in which he actively pursued the role of political poet.

My interest in these matters began with an attempt to see whether the techniques and insights that scholars and critics have developed in reading sacred metaphor in devotional poetry of the earlier seventeenth century and in analyzing Milton's use of Scripture would illuminate the poetry of King, Cleveland, Marvell, and Dryden. The answer, already implied —yes, but a qualified yes—is set forth in the pages that follow. I have tried, first of all, to clarify the language that might be used in discussing scriptural metaphor in Dryden's poetry and to show how typology differs in political and devotional contexts. Then, before discussing Dryden's major political poems, I have surveyed the extent and variety of typology in public literature to suggest the immediate and full historical context for Dryden's use of sacred metaphor and to chart some of the ways in which the use of scriptural metaphor changed during the seventeenth century. This combination of literary history and critical analysis will, I hope, serve as a useful commentary on Dryden's political poetry and the cultural traditions from which he wrote and will suggest how Dryden—like Virgil and Horace, Marvell and Pope—rendered universal the transient issues and partisan stances of the political poet.

It is a pleasure to acknowledge the help that I have received in writing this book. My thanks are due to the Woodrow Wilson Foundation for support in graduate school and for a dissertation year fellowship; to the Charles Phelps Taft Foundation for a postdoctoral fellowship during which revisions on the manuscript were completed; to the Taft Foundation and to the Washington University Graduate School for aid in the preparation of the typescript; to Washington University for a generous subvention toward the cost of publication; to William Conway and the staff of the William Andrews Clark Library for their repeated hospitality; to Marion L. Kesselring of the Brown University Library, who helped in many ways when I began my reading; to the staff of the Huntington Library; and to Professor Curt A. Zimansky, editor of *Philological Quarterly,* for permission to reprint chapter 3 of this book, which appeared in volume L, number 4, and for his comments on the chapter.

My work has received generous attention from teachers and friends. Professor Edward Bloom and Professor David Underdown constructively criticized an early draft; Professor Sacvan Bercovitch made numerous helpful suggestions, especially for chapter 1; Professor William Madsen commented on my theoretical discussion of typology; and Donald Mull helped with stylistic revisions. My greatest debt is to Professor Barbara Lewalski, who directed this study as a dissertation and whose guidance and encouragement throughout my work have been invaluable; for her learning and generous interest I am deeply grateful.

The most difficult obligation to acknowledge fully is that to my wife for her constant help and support; for that, and for much more, this book is dedicated to her.

DRYDEN'S POLITICAL POETRY

1 THE TERMS OF METAPHORICAL HISTORY

The use of the term *typology* in a discussion of seventeenth-century poetry is beset with critical hazards. The long history of typological exegesis, the varied applications of typology by the church fathers, the close relationship that typology bears to allegory and other methods of biblical interpretation, and the variety of devotional and political applications of biblical typology in seventeenth-century literature have undoubtedly given the word more meanings than it can hold at one time. Moreover, *type* is often used with its familiar meaning of "kind," or "distinguishing example," in reference to biblical and historical characters; Nimrod, for example, is frequently cited as type of the tyrant.[1] To confuse further these legitimate sources of the term's complexity, recent typological criticism has given *type* and *typology* a currency in critical writing that has resulted in casual, if not ill-advised, usage.[2] In some instances *typology* is so loosely used that it fails to retain the shape necessary for definition; in others, *typology* is so closely defined or applied with such rigid particularity as to violate the very flexibility that distinguishes the use of typology by poets and divines of a given age. The result in either case is a confusion in language and thought that produces noticeable anxiety about the limits of typological criticism. Indeed, one reviewer of a recent book on the figuralism of the *Divine Comedy* closes her critique with the wish that the author had excluded from his discussion even the term *typology* itself.[3]

A basic definition of *typology* for the discussion of Dryden's poetry must be two-fold: historical and critical. In order to treat the typological imagery in Dryden's poetry with historical accuracy, the nature and applications of Renaissance figuralism must be considered.[4] But having established the historical context so that the scriptural types and their seventeenth-century significance can be identified, the particular complex of meaning involved in the type must be related to, yet distinguished from, the historical analogue and the allegorical figure of moral or religious significance.

Typology is the name given to the practice of scriptural exegesis that reads in various Old Testament figures, events, and institutions a Christian, if not specifically christological, meaning.[5] To clarify this distinction, which will be important to an understanding of the political applications of typology, it should be noted that Christology in devotional or exegetical application focuses attention on the person or attributes of Christ. Christocentric typology aims at uncovering or clarifying relationships between Old Testament figures and events and the person of the Redeemer, but not all typological exegesis, especially after the Reformation, is christocentric. The impact of the Protestant movement of covenant theology with its emphasis on national election was, in part, to focus the prophetic (antitypical) significance of Old Testament types on nonchristological terms.[6] The New Canaan or New Jerusalem of Christian eschatology was seen as fulfilling the Israelite nation, and the Last Judgment and the millennium became antitypes for the Israelite judges, the Davidic kingdom, or the Christian commonwealth.[7] Typology, then, according to modern biblical scholars, is an attempt to establish historical connections between events, persons, and institutions in the Old Testament (types) and similar events, persons, and institutions in the New Testament (antitypes).[8] Building on this definition and following the work of Erich Auerbach,[9] literary scholars and critics have pointed to the mutual historicity that encompasses the events typologically related as the primary characteristic of figuralism in literary texts.

The Origins and Development of Typology

Typological exegesis as practiced by the early Latin church fathers, and then inherited by and transformed in western

European medieval and Renaissance commentary and literature, began with the apostolic use of typology to show Old Testament prophecy fulfilled in Christ and to demonstrate congruency between the history of God's people under the Law and the fate of the elect nation under the Dispensation of Mercy. Although the concept of typology must be located in the Old Testament and in pre-Christian rabbinic commentary, and *figure* and *type* can be traced even to Terence and Plautus, the examples of Christian typological reading found in the New Testament provide the soundest basis for a discussion of seventeenth-century typology, since the Scriptures were of central importance to English Renaissance thought and literary expression.[10]

The major Old Testament personages and events that were read figurally by the Apostles appear in a variety of New Testament contexts.[11] Adam is referred to twice as a type of Christ: in Romans 5:14 he is the "figure of him that was to come," and according to 1 Corinthians 15:45, "the first man Adam was made a living soul; the last Adam *was made* a quickening spirit." Noah is read typologically in his person and in his history in 1 Peter 3:20–21: "the longsuffering of God waited in the days of Noah, while the ark was a preparing, wherein few, that is, eight souls were saved by water. The like figure whereunto *even* baptism doth also now save us (not the putting away of the filth of the flesh, but the answer of a good conscience toward God,) by the resurrection of Jesus Christ." In Matthew 17:1–5 Moses on Mount Sinai prefigures Christ's transfiguration, and John 3:14–17 compares Moses lifting the brazen serpent in the wilderness to the Son of man being lifted up to save the world. Solomon in Matthew 12:42 is suggested as a type of Christ in his wisdom, and Jonah in Matthew 12:40 is read figurally in his whale burial: "For as Jonas was three days and three nights in the whale's belly; so shall the Son of man be three days and three nights in the heart of the earth."

In addition to Old Testament individuals, groups or orders of Old Testament peoples were at times interpreted figurally in the New Testament. The whole nation of the Jews, for example, is interpreted as a figure of the Church in Galatians 6:16, and the Old Testament offices of prophet, priest, and king are in different passages associated with their fulfillment in Christ. Finally, Old Testament historical events were read typologically in the New Testament. The deliverance out of slavery is interpreted in Matthew 2:14–15 as a figure that foretokened God's calling forth of his son from Egypt; in 1 Corinthians 10:1, 2, 5, the passage through the Red Sea and the march through the wilderness are referred to as types of Christian spiritual experience; and the Land of Canaan, toward which the Israelites traveled, is interpreted by Paul in Hebrews 11:16 as a figure of heaven. Old Testament persons and events are used variously as types of Christ in his offices, death, and resurrection; as foreshadowings of the Church; as figures of Christian spiritual experience; and as eschatological prophecies. This sampling should indicate that the New Testament provides suggestions of, and a basis for, ways in which the Old Testament could be read figurally; but the basis itself, especially when placed against the systematic handling of types in the seventeenth-century typology manuals, is in no way exhaustive. Even the Pauline Epistles, which abound in Old Testament references, do not explore intensively the possibilities of figurative reading or offer the rigorous schematization of Old Testament person and event that distinguish, in different ways, patristic commentary and seventeenth-century typology.

The history of exegetical traditions from the church fathers to the seventeenth century is a highly complex subject, yet before turning to definitions of typology in specific seventeenth-century texts, certain lines of continuity between medieval and Reformation commentary should be suggested.[12] This continuity can be most effectively outlined with reference to the two dominant modes of Christian historiography that reach from Augustine through the Reformation: the essentially ahistorical, spiritual understanding of history as a record of individual salvation that is very influential in the Middle Ages and informs certain aspects of Calvinist theology;[13] and the progressivist theories of Eusebius and Orosius that find expression in the prophesies of Joachim and

Joachimist works of the later Middle Ages and that culminate in Luther's progressivist-millenarian historiography as well as in the chiliasm of the millenarian divines of seventeenth-century England and New England.[14]

Augustine's framing of salvational history in terms of the progress of the individual soul toward the eternal figure of the Heavenly Jerusalem finds expression not only in medieval devotional art but also in the devotional literature of seventeenth-century England, for example, Donne's *Hymns* and *Holy Sonnets,* Herbert's *Temple,* or Bunyan's *Pilgrim's Progress*. In such contexts, Old Testament history "types out an essentially private eschatological experience." [15] Rather than a progressive account of human institutions, history was for Augustine the operation of God in time, a one-directional, teleological process whose one goal was the salvation of the individual: "In effect, Augustine denies the applicability of typological exegesis to the public, social life of men." [16] The political application of typology found a basis in the progressivist theory of Christian history, in which the city or nation became an expression of God's ordering of history: Israel in the Old Testament; Rome in the early medieval histories of Eusebius and Orosius; Protestant England for the Elizabethans; the English Commonwealth for Puritan divines; and New England for many of the English dissenters who came to America.

The idea of corporate or federal election that built upon the temporal or provisional covenant (Jer. 31:32), as distinct from the perpetual covenant (Jer. 31:31, 33), was given further impetus in Reformation covenant theology, which stressed, for the millenarian, the role of Old Testament Israel as a prefiguration of a nation or people destined to lead the world into the millennium. In less radical circles, and indeed in most of the political poetry with which this study is concerned, the present-day elect were seen not as the antitypical fulfillment of Old Testament Israel but rather as a correlative of that nation.[17] Both covenanted nations lived in the flow of historical time, but through their special relationship with each other and through their covenanted relationship with

God, history became sacred history. It is this public, federal
sense that is here reserved for the term *sacred history*.

The Seventeenth-Century Exegetical Definition of Typology

Ancient and medieval typology can serve as a frame for ex-
amining exegetical modes in Renaissance England, but an
understanding of specific practices in Dryden's own time can
be gained only from a sampling of exegetical texts that represent the interpretive practices of a theologically diverse
group of commentators. Samuel Mather's *Figures or Types of
the Old Testament*, William Guild's *Moses unveiled*, and
John Brinsley's *Mystical Brasen Serpent* offer such a sampling.[18] Mather was a Congregationalist divine who was sus-
pended at the Restoration for sermons against the revival of
ceremonies in the Church of England and was in 1662 ejected
by the Uniformity Act. Guild dedicated *Moses unveiled* to
Lancelot Andrewes and was, through the influence of the
dean of Winchester, made a chaplain to Charles I. Brinsley,
in ways the most puzzling of the three, was a Puritan divine
and nephew of Bishop Hall. Though *The Mystical Brasen
Serpent* in its devotional emphasis is more reminiscent of the
works of Anglican divines and poets, Brinsley apparently was
not of that theological bent. At the Restoration he was ejected
for refusing the terms of conformity.[19] *The Figures or Types*
offers a straightforward, analytical description of what a type
is and what it does. *Moses unveiled* gives a more imaginative
rendering of typology in terms of a distinction between the
shadows of the Old Dispensation and the "true Phosphorous"
of the New. The third text, *The Mystical Brasen Serpent*,
makes a useful distinction between typology and analogy.

Mather begins his definition of *type* with the logical choice
of a verse from the New Testament: "*a Type is a Shadow of
good things to come*, Hebr. 10. 1"; he proceeds from that text
to the systematic handling of types that characterizes his

method throughout the lengthy volume, as it does the sys-
tematization of typology in a large number of seventeenth-
century exegetical manuals. From Paul's definition Mather
turns to the "Description of a *Type*, what it is" and proceeds
to subdivide the description according to its contents:

1. There is some outward or sensible thing that represents some higher thing.
2. There is the thing represented thereby, which is *good
things to come*, which we call the *Antitype*.
3. There is the work of the *Type*, which is to *shadow
forth* or represent these *future good things*.[20]

From the description of what the type is, Mather proceeds by
analogy to what the type does. As a shadow reflects the body,
so, for the Old Testament elect, do the types adumbrate and
represent Christ and his benefits.

In thus defining the type, Mather dwells upon its instruc-
tive function in Scripture: "to enlighten and inform their Un-
derstandings, and to strengthen and confirm their Faith in
him"; [21] and it is especially this persuasive function that commonly informs devotional and political uses of scriptural
typology. In devotional typology the center of instruction or
persuasion is Christ in his sacrificial and salvific offices, while
in political typology the center of instruction or persuasion
has shifted from the devotional antitype to the political or
historical correlative type. Recapitulating, Mather calls the
type a "shadow of good things to come, . . . some outward or
sensible thing ordained of God under the Old Testament, to
represent and hold forth something of Christ in the New, . . .
an instituted resemblance of Gospel-Truths and Mysteries,
. . . a Sign holding forth Christ, or something of Christ in the
New Testament." He concludes by saying, "You see it comes
all to one scope; and indeed all the Descriptions that our
Divines have given of it are to this effect, they are all to the
same scope with this of the Apostle; *a Shadow of good things
to come*." [22] This rather hedging coda, which falls back on the
safety of the very general New Testament definition, should
give some indication that the seventeenth-century definition

of *type* admitted of wide variation and that even the rigorous systematizing and subdividing intellect of the manual writer is forced finally to come to the definition from several directions.

William Guild, author of two typology manuals, expresses in the dedicatory epistle to *Moses unveiled* the same understanding of the type. Both Guild and Mather define it as a foreshadowing in the Old Testament of Christ in his offices and functions in the New Testament, but Guild's dedicatory epistle suggests the kind of imagistic language, abounding in the poetic applications of typology, that could accompany the straightforward description of types:

> As in the Creation darkness went before light, or as the dawning precedes the brightness of the day, and as *Joseph* obscurely at first behaved himself unto his Brethren, and *Moses* covered with a veil stood before the people: Even so *(right Reverend)* in the detection of the glorious work of mans Redemption, mystical promises went before mercifull performance, dark shaddows were the fore-runners of that bright substance, obscure types were harbingers to that glorious Anty-type the Messiah. . . . So that as folded in swadling clouts, and lying in a Crib, he was seen and shewn unto the Wise-men that came from the East; so involved in typical Ordinances, and lurking under shadowish signs, he was offered and exhibited unto the Jews that saw his day but a far off; the ecclipsed and dimme light of the Moon (as it were) as yet only glimmering, or the twinkling brightness of starry Lamps, as yet only dazedly glistering: Untill the true *Phosphorous,* that glorious Sun himself did arise in the Horizon of our Humanity.[23]

Finally, John Brinsley's *Mystical Brasen Serpent,* a commentary on John 3:14–15, offers a definition of *type* by way of a distinction that the author makes between type and similitude:

> And the like we may say of this *Brasen Serpent.* It was to the Israelites both a *Medicine,* and a *Mystery.* Having

in it a *Medicinall* use for the curing of their Bodies; a *Mysticall* use, for the representing of Christ to them, by whom their *Souls* might be cured and saved.

And of such use our Saviour here maketh it; bringing it in not barely by way of *Similitude* and resemblance; but as a *Type* and Figure, purposely destinated and appointed to point to himself.[24]

Brinsley's distinction between type and similitude is important both for what it tells about the quality or intensity of the relationship that typology activates and for the express connection that types, which are "purposely destinated and appointed," have with each other and with the antitype through the place that they share in sacred history. Moreover, Brinsley's distinction is essential to the study of typological imagery in Dryden's poetry. It not only explains the important relationship between sacred history and typology but also points out the difference between the analogue and the type. The analogue is extrinsically related to another object; the type is intrinsically related to the antitype ("destinated and appointed"), a figure whose special meaning relies on the fact that it is part of sacred history. In the political use of typology, Old Testament figures and events become correlatives of contemporary figures and events. Thus, in his political poetry, Dryden's presentation of Restoration history as sacred history is reinforced by the use of the language and imagery of typology, and the typological bond between, for example, Charles II and David is strengthened by Dryden's setting that relationship in the context of sacred history.

Though the passages from Mather, Guild, and Brinsley give some idea of the seventeenth-century definition of *typology*, the rigorous application of this definition to the text of the Old Testament can be appreciated only by a direct sampling from one of the manuals. Mather's *Figures or Types* is a characteristic production and will suggest the scope of the typology manual as well as the intense detail with which the more important Old Testament figures and events were treated. Mather divides his book into a number of "Gospels" and under each makes numerous subdivisions. Following 674 pages of exegesis on a variety of typical persons, events, and objects, Mather provides his reader with a "brief view and recapitulation of all the Types." [25] Not only is the manual impressive in scope but the detail with which some of the individual types are handled is nothing less than exhaustive. Noah, for example, is treated for nine quarto pages, not only as a type of Christ in his saving of the remnant, but also with reference to the "divers *real Types* belonging to the History of *this personal Type*." Under the heading *"real Types,"* the term Mather uses to refer to objects from the Old Testament as distinct from Old Testament offices or persons, he includes the ark, the Deluge, the waters, Noah's "acceptable Sacrifice," the Lord's covenant with Noah, and "the Rainbow the Sign thereof." Under the analysis of the ways in which the ark typified the Church, Mather offers a reading of the spiritual significance of the ark's pump, sails, wind, rudder, door, window, rooms or chambers, and stories. [26]

The breadth and detail of Mather's exegesis suggest the kind of typological analysis that was available to the mid-seventeenth-century reading public; the printed format and the number of times the book was issued suggest the extent of the manual's distribution and the general nature of its audience. Between 1683 and 1700 *Figures or Types* went through three printings, all in quarto format, and was issued again in 1705. (*Moses unveiled* went through two printings before 1700 in an octavo format; and John Bunyan's *Solomon's Temple Spiritualized* went through three printings between 1688 and 1698 in a duodecimo format.) *Figures or Types,* like the other typology manuals, is not a sophisticated theological treatise but an elementary, if intensively detailed, collection of figural readings.

The typology manuals of the Puritan divines were not, of course, the only source of figural exegesis. Commentaries on the Old and New Testament—among them Isaac Penington's *Expositions with observations sometimes, on severall scriptures* (1656); John Weemse's *Exercitations Divine* (1632); John Pearson's *Exposition of the Creed* (1662); William Gouge's *Learned and very useful commentary on the whole Epistle to the Hebrews* (1655); Francis Roberts's *Mysterium and Medulla Bibliorum* (1657); and John Davenport's *Knowl-edge of Christ indispensably required of all men that would be saved* (1653) [27]—are filled with typological readings of verses selected from the Old Testament, expansions on passages from the Apostles that treat the Old Testament figurally, and standard exegetical readings of the basic Old Testament characters and events.

From the evidence surveyed, which is by no means exhaustive, it should be evident that typological exegesis was very common in seventeenth-century England and that examples of individual typological readings were available in numerous and easily accessible volumes.[28] Indeed, both lettered and unlettered Englishmen of the seventeenth century could hardly have avoided contact with typological interpretation of the Old Testament; and it is not difficult to assume that Dryden, who displays in *Religio Laici* and *The Hind and the Panther* considerable learning and acumen in his discussion of theology, was more than familiar with so standard a method of biblical reading as typology. Also from Dryden's discussion of traditional exegesis in the religious poems and his mention of Origen, as well as from the interesting suggestion that he owned a manuscript copy of Peter of Lombard's commentary on Paul's Epistles, it can be assumed that Dryden was, if not steeped in, at least familiar with patristic exegesis.[29] Such an assumption is not necessary, however, in order to argue that Dryden was well versed in the methods of typological exegesis common to the seventeenth century. The sermons that he heard and read, the Bible that he used at Cambridge,[30] as well as the poems with which he was demonstrably familiar, contain abundant evidence that figural imagery was common in the seventeenth century.

Devotional Typology

Sermons preached in the Anglican church before the civil war and after the Restoration, as well as sermons of dissenting ministers, illustrate the widespread devotional and political application of typology. Donne's sermon on Psalm 38:2, "For thine arrowes stick fast in me, and thy hand presseth me sore," provides a vivid and persuasive handling of typology in the personal and devotional mode. The sermon concludes with Donne's use of the scriptural text to draw together past and present, engaging through the typological perspective both Old Testament subject and seventeenth-century reader in the Christian paradigm:

> To end all, and to dismisse you with such a re-collection, as you may carry away with you; literally, primarily, this text concerns *David:* He by *tentations* to sin, by *tribulations* for sin, by *comminations,* and *increpations* upon sin, was bodily, and ghostly become a quiver of arrows of all sorts; they *stook,* and stook *fast,* and stook *full* in him, in *all* him. The Psalm hath a *retrospect* too, it looks back to *Adam,* and to every particular man in his loines, and so, *Davids* case is our case, and all these arrowes stick in all us. But the Psalm and the text hath also a *prospect,* and hath a *propheticall* relation from *David* to our Saviour Christ Jesus. And of him, and of the multiplicity of these arrows upon him in the exinanition, and evacuation of himself, in this world for us, have many of the *Ancients* interpreted these words literally, and as in their first and primary signification; Turne we therefore to *him,* before we goe, and he shall return home with us.[31]

The typological interpretation of the psalm links David backward to Adam, forward to Christ, and forward again to all men. Donne, unlike the *"Ancients"* who took Christ to be the literal sense of David, accepts the primary and literal meaning of the Old Testament psalmist; but together with the Old Testament significance of David's words, Donne can read a prophetic meaning, and it is ultimately this prophetic sense that contains the most urgent meaning for the audience of Donne's sermon. The prophetic sense of the verse directs the audience to "our Saviour Christ Jesus," to those arrows that stick fast in him, and to the salvific meaning of his suffering. The typology is christocentric and devotional in nature; the figural meaning of the Scripture is invoked, as Mather would have it, to "enlighten and inform," to "strengthen and confirm their Faith in him." Donne recognizes the moral authority that David's words have as part of sacred history, but more important for Donne's persuasive intent, they are a *"Shadow of good things to come";* he sends his audience home with the recollection of the literal and typological meaning of David's words, but it is the typological perspective that turns the listener back to Christ: "Turne we therefore to *him,* before we goe, and he shall return home with us."

Lancelot Andrewes, in an Easter sermon preached on John 20:11–17, uses typology in explicating the twelfth verse, "And saw two Angels in white, sitting, the one at the head, the other at the feet, where the body of Jesus had lain." Though less elaborate than Donne's reading, Andrewes's sermon invokes the figural perspective with the same devotional intent. Beginning with the words "in white," Andrewes explicates:

> *In white,* and *sitting:* As the colour, of joy: so, the situation, of rest. So wee say, *Sit downe,* and *rest.* And so, is the grave made by this mornings worke, a place of *rest. Rest,* not from our labours onely, so doe the beasts rest when they die: But, as it is in the 16. Psalme (a Psalme of the *resurrection*) a *rest in hope*; hope, of rising againe, the members in the vertue of their head, who this day is risen. So, to enter into the rest, which yet *remaineth for the people of God,* even the Sabbath eternall.
>
> *Sitting,* and in this order *sitting, at the head, one; at the feet, another, where His body had lyen.*
>
> Which order may well referre to *Christ* himselfe, whose body was the true *Arke* indeed, *In which it pleased the Godhead to dwell bodily,* and is therefore heere betweene two *Angels,* as was the *Arke* (the type of it) *betweene the two Cherubims.*[32]

In the first paragraph Andrewes shows how David's *"rest in hope"* is fulfilled through Christ's rest in the grave and resurrection; in turn he alludes to the Jewish Sabbath as a type, or promise, of the final rest that "yet *remaineth for the people of God.*" The extension of the typological relationship to include the *"people of God"* is an allusion to the Israelites and their promised rest in Canaan as an eschatological type of the blessed state that the true Israel of God will enjoy at the end of time. Both David's *"rest in hope"* and Israel's rest in Canaan are activated through Christ's sacrificial rest in the grave, which promises eternal rest for the believer.

In the second paragraph Andrewes uses the familiar scriptural type of the ark as a foreshadowing of Christ's body, "the true Arke indeed." In Exodus 25:22 the ark in the tabernacle is promised by God as the place where he will meet the Israelites, the sign of his protective and guiding power among the chosen people. Christ as the true ark fulfills the promise of God's continued presence among all his Israelites. The scriptural type is common, as is the meaning that Andrewes assigns to it. The emphasis is clearly devotional: the scriptural types are a promise of redemption to the Christian believer.

Political Typology

Devotional typology in both seventeenth-century prose and poetry has received considerable attention, as has the relationship between medieval devotional art with its uses of christocentric typology and seventeenth-century religious expression.[33] But the idea that political as well as devotional matters could be and were informed by sacred history and figural imagery and that in fact political uses of typology were widespread in the seventeenth century has not been adequately explored. Less attention has been given to typological imagery in political poetry, no doubt because many of the political poems of the seventeenth century, like much of the occasional verse of any age, are of less than compelling interest as literature. Yet the seventeenth century is noticeably rich in occasional poetry of a very high order. Not only is there interesting occasional verse by literary amateurs, but most of the

great poets of the century wrote poetry of an occasional and
political nature. Donne, Jonson, Herrick, Carew, King, Milton, Marvell, Cleveland, and, of course, Dryden wrote occasional verse; and King, Marvell, Cleveland, and Dryden made
significant use of typological imagery in treating of public affairs. But the neglect of political uses of typology is more importantly related to the seeming difficulty in making a mean-
ingful connection between devotional and political typology
—between a use of scriptural types to reveal gospel truths and
teach a salvific message and the obviously partisan, and seem-
ingly transient, affairs with which political poets deal. Even
more specifically, it has seemed difficult to many critics to
make a connection between the highly personal and intensely
serious use of Scripture in the poetry of Donne, Herbert, or
Milton and the relatively worldly, or what one critic has
called the "fustian," use of sacred history to praise monarchs
and men of public affairs. And, indeed, the connection is difficult to make; it is in fact the wrong one to make, since the
use of scriptural typology in Marvell and Dryden does not develop out of the techniques and assumptions that Donne and
Herbert had exemplified earlier in the century in their use of
figural imagery. Rather, political typology grows from a distinct literary tradition, finding a base in progressivist historiography and a hermeneutical foundation in Luther's Reformation theology rather than in medieval christocentric theology.

The interaction of medieval hermeneutics and devotional
typology and its relationship to the interaction of Reformation exegetical theory and the political applications of typology is a complex subject; yet a basic distinction between
medieval and Reformation commentary can be made with
reference to their respective emphasis on the importance of
the Old Testament. The medieval exegetical approach to the
Old Testament is almost solely figural: "Indeed, one would
not exaggerate too much in saying that, in this view, redemptive history really begins only with the coming of Christ.
Everything before it is *figura*." [34] Donne's sermon on 1 Corinthians 15:26, "The last enemie that shall be destroyed, is

death," nicely supports that analysis of the medieval exegetical approach to the Old Testament:

> Upon that pious ground that all Scriptures were written for us, as we are Christians, that all Scriptures conduce to the proofe of Christ, and of the Christian state, it is the ordinary manner of the Fathers to make all that *David* speaks historically of himselfe, and all that the Prophet speaks futurely of the Jews, if those places may be referred to Christ, to referre them to Christ primarily, and but by reflection, and in a second consideration upon *David,* or upon the Jews.[35]

The basic and most important change that Reformation theology made in Old Testament interpretation is that, rather than regarding the coming of Christ as the center of Scripture, it emphasized the moral authority of the Old Testament.[36] Without denying the significance or the impact of Calvin's thought on English Reformation theology, this change is surely attributable to Luther's influential millenarian theories rather than to Calvin's christocentric outlook. Israel's Babylonian captivity, for example, signified for Calvin the bondage of sin; like Augustine, Calvin denied the possibility of a temporal commitment on God's part.[37] Luther, however, "attached a concrete, wordly import to the captivity; seeking a correlation between prophecies and contemporary events in order to answer the Roman Catholic objections to the Reformation, he found in the New Covenant an adumbration of man's temporal progress."[38] The English Puritans did not learn chiliasm from Calvin: "in England it was first Wyclif, then Bale and Bullinger, who developed the idea that the Book of Revelation foretold the destruction of the Romish Antichrist"; moreover, it was John Foxe who conditioned English Protestants to a belief in the "historic mission of their role."[39]

Historically the important break comes in Luther's commentary on the Psalms, in which the "actual appearance of Christ in history . . . is no longer determinative for theological value to be accorded to the Old Testament text, and to the historical situation of the Old Testament People." [40] The medieval identification between the faithful and Christ is replaced, in Luther's new scheme, by an identification between the two elect nations: the Old Testament faithful and the present-day elect. With this new identification comes the notion of correlative typology, which is the basis for the connection that Dryden and so many other seventeenth-century poets and divines make between England and Israel, between the English and the Israelites. The steps from Luther to Dryden are any number of sermons and political poems that make the connection a traditional way of understanding English history. Under the historical pressure of the conflict between Protestant England and the Catholic powers abroad, the identification of the faithful Anglican church with faithful Israel easily takes on a national coloring at the close of the sixteenth century. The Protestant faithful become identified with the English people, while the enemies of England become identified with the enemies of Old Testament Israel.

The basic identification between England and Israel has a number of interesting ramifications. Elizabeth, for example, is celebrated at the turn of the century as an English David who protected her people from the Romish Edomites.[41] The international division between the elect and the enemies of God's people, however, becomes internalized in the course of the seventeenth century as the political division between king and Parliament grows and draws the Anglican church and dissenting ministers into political opposition. From this point it should be clear how politics, religion, and literature interact to create the identities that Dryden will eventually use in his political poetry, a use that culminates in *Absalom and Achitophel.*

The identification of England with Israel and the treatment of their histories as correlative records of the mercies and punishments God visited upon his chosen people is one of the most familiar examples of correlative typology in seventeenth-century political literature; it is an identification on which the political interpretation of England's sacred history rests. In his sermon *Hezekia's Recoverie* (1626) Robert Harris declares, "I cannot read what *Moses* said to his Israel, and not make it ours. Happy art thou O England, who is like unto thee, O people saved by the Lord? &c. *Deut.* 33.29. For what Nation is there so great, who hath God so nigh unto them (the onely glory of a Nation) as the Lord our God is, in all things that wee call upon him for?" [42] But toward the close of the century, the sacred history of Israel is often invoked, not to emphasize the blessed condition that both chosen peoples have enjoyed but, rather, to underline the rightful vengeance that God has visited upon both nations in the past. John Turner's *Two Sermons*, preached in January 1687, recounts this correlative history of unhappiness to remind the English how the tragedies of anarchy and confusion wrought by the civil war resemble those that Israel suffered after the death of Samson, *"when there was no King in Israel, but every Man did that which was right in his own Eyes. The Consequence of which, was First, the Destruction of the National Religion of the Jews, and the crumbling it into numberless Parties and Distinctions, as appears immediately by the Story of Micah."* [43]

More specific relationships between men and events in these two sacred histories can be found in the occasional verse produced for coronations and funerals of the monarchs. Such poems use both the basic analogy between England and Israel and more specific identifications between Old Testament and contemporary history.[44] King and people, as numerous poetic examples suggest, share in the figural relationship between England and Israel. It is this same shared relationship that Edward Boteler emphasizes in his coronation sermon for Charles II, *Gods Goodnesse in Crowning the King.*[45] For Boteler, the English have suffered an Egyptian bondage under the pharoah Cromwell, and God will deliver them through the salvific instrument of a king. The king as head of the nation rules as Christ rules over the Church. English history is read as sacred history in these texts; the nation prospers and suffers like the Israelites of old; the king is at once David and a type of Christ.

The typological relationship between the king and Christ is, along with the relationship between England and Israel, a basic component in seventeenth-century political typology. Reformation hermeneutical theory permits of the fundamental connection between the Old and New Testament faithful, but medieval political theology is the source of Christomimesis: the typological identification of the king with Christ. The Christ-imitating king is the " 'mediator' between heaven and earth," the " 'actor' or 'impersonator' of Christ— who on the terrestrial stage presented the living image of the two-natured God." Such "language of christological exemplarism . . . was used throughout to proclaim the king a *typus Christi*." [46] Medieval political theology is, of course, something very different from Restoration politics; yet the language deriving from medieval political theory seems to have had a remarkable staying power and in fact was given new life by events in seventeenth-century history. In *The Holy State* (1642) Thomas Fuller begins his essay *The King* with the words "He is a mortall God." [47] But the events surrounding, and the literature lamenting, the death of Charles I in 1649 gave special impetus to the typology of kingship. Charles's execution was frequently conflated with the Crucifixion, and the language of thorns and crosses is particularly noticeable in the literature on the king's death. If Dryden is one of the last poets who can celebrate the king as a "type of him above" [48] and if the seventeenth century is the last age in which the parallel can be drawn between the position of God in the universe and the position of the monarch in the kingdom, both analogies are drawn frequently and vigorously before the political and religious context changes so that these parallels can no longer be observed.

Political typology shares a language with typological exegesis of the Old Testament and with the devotional uses of typology; but unlike the former, its goal is not to show all Scripture teaching faith, love, and hope; and unlike the latter, its contemporary application is not to the moral state of the believer. Rather, the intent of political typology is to

show the nation and the national leader participating in the
sanctity of God's providence. The occasional poet or divine
using scriptural types for a political purpose focuses on the
condition of the contemporary correlative type and uses the
relationship between Old Testament and contemporary history to emphasize the ways in which the events in the record of
God's people are repeated and recapitulated throughout time.
The contemporary person and event share in the sacred history
of the past, and both correlative types participate in the eternal
paradigm that is the model of Christian history. Charles and
David in their divine anointment, England and Israel in their
special promise, are correlative types participating in sacred
history. Although the relationship between correlative types
can be elaborated without reference to the third, antitypical
term, that linking element can often be felt and is often invoked. Both Old Testament and contemporary events retain
their literal and historical primacy, and both are enriched by
the relationship that they bear to the implied or stated antitype.

Biblical imagery and scriptural allusions in Dryden's poetry
have not, of course, gone unnoticed. Why, then, is it necessary or even useful to consider the figural perspective of such
imagery when the scriptural parallels have already been considered in analogical and allegorical terms? First, as the material in this chapter demonstrates, *type* and *figure* are tech-
nical terms that have a specific use and definition in Dryden's
age. The modern term *typological image,* when used to describe a particular image in a seventeenth-century text, implies a specific relationship that the example under discussion
bears to a literary and exegetical tradition. Neither *analogy*
nor *allegory* necessarily asks the reader to consider the specific
biblical image within the tradition of political or devotional
typology; nor will *analogy* or *allegory* lead the reader to investigate the ways in which the specific scriptural image might
connect to the general context of sacred history or to the
typological meaning that was assigned by contemporary
exegesis to the Old Testament person or event. The use of

type and the description *typological image,* as distinguished from *allegory* or *analogy,* however, can be defended on even more specific grounds.

Typology and Allegory

Before dealing with the critical distinctions between typology and allegory in Renaissance literary texts, it should be noted that in the exegetical language of medieval commentary *allegory* was used to signify what the later seventeenth-century commentators designated *typic* or *typical.*[49] This medieval use of *allegory* persists in some Renaissance commentary and can be found, for example, in the early seventeenth-century treatise *The Art of Prophecying* (1631) by William Perkins.[50] In the schematization of typological reading that occurs in the middle and later seventeenth century, however, *allegory* as a term for the typological reading drops out of the exegetes' vocabulary, so that a clarification of language can be noticed in the manuals that were published in the later seventeenth century. For this reason and for obvious reasons of clarity, *allegory* will be treated as a term that designates a literary form and *typology* will be reserved for the exegetical meaning that refers to the Christian interpretation of Old Testament events.

The definition of allegory as a narrative technique in Renaissance literature is basically contained in the etymology of the word. The Greek words from which the Latin *allegoria* is borrowed are ἀλληγορία, "a description of one thing under the image of another," and ἀλληγορεῖν, "to speak so as to imply something else." [51] In Renaissance allegories these come to mean that one narrative, invented or borrowed, is made to serve as a vehicle for a second story or set of terms.[52] The two narratives are not of equal importance to the writer nor are they meant to be of equal importance to the reader; one narrative is concealed in another, and it is the concealed or shadowed narrative that carries the moral significance of the first.

Thus Spenser in his "Letter to Raleigh" clearly distinguishes between the moral and fictive levels of his work and suggests the importance of the moral over the fictive level: "To some I know this Methode will seeme displeasaunt, which had rather have good discipline delivered plainly in way of precepts, or sermoned at large, as they use, then thus clowdily enwrapped in Allegoricall devices." [53]

Some readers have, indeed, objected to the more than thirty thousand lines of "clowdily enwrapped" moral precept, but none until recently has doubted that the energies of reader and critic must be steadily aimed at unwrapping the "real" meaning of *The Faerie Queene*. Similarly, Sidney makes the connection between fable and the allegorical techniques of narrative when he describes the poet as a popular philosopher "whose pretty Allegories, stealing under the formall tales of Beastes, make many, more beastly then Beasts, begin to heare the sound of vertue from these dumbe speakers." [54] Thomas Wilson, in *The Arte of Rhetorique,* describes allegory as a metaphor used throughout an oration and likens it to "darke devised sentences." [55] While Puttenham puts matters: "For what else is your *Metaphor* but an inversion of sence by transport; your *allegorie* by a duplicitie of meaning . . . seeking to inveigle and appassionate the mind." [56] Addison, at the close of the seventeenth century, points to the same disjunction between the fictive and moral components of allegorical tales:

> But now the Mystick Tale, that pleas'd of Yore,
> Can Charm an understanding Age no more;
> The long-spun Allegories fulsom grow,
> While the dull Moral lies too plain below.[57]

These historical definitions emphasize the clearly fictive element attached to the concept of allegory by Renaissance criticism and by Renaissance uses of allegory as a narrative device. The historical truth of the allegorical device is not a matter of importance. Thus beast fables, legends, romances, and invented narrative perfectly suit, and are most commonly used as, the fictive term of allegorical narratives. By contrast, both terms in the figural or typological relationship are literal and are historically true; neither of the terms is expendable or arbitrary. In scriptural typology both terms have the authority of sacred history; in the political uses of typology the mutual sanctity of the correlative types, their mutual truth as part of sacred history, is basic to the purpose of the political poet. "Since in figural interpretation one thing stands for another, . . . figural interpretation is 'allegorical' in the widest sense. But it differs from most of the allegorical forms known to us by the historicity both of the sign and what it signifies. Most of the allegories we find in literature or art represent a virtue (e.g., wisdom), or a passion (jealousy), an institution (justice), or at most a very general synthesis of historical phenomena (peace, the fatherland)—never a definite event in its full historicity." [58] Allegory, then, by definition and example drawn from Renaissance critical and imaginative literature involves two terms, only one of which is vested with truth or moral import. In typology, both type and antitype, and both Old Testament and contemporary correlative types, are rooted in truth; the relationship between types in exegesis and in literature depends on the author's commitment to, and the audience's acceptance of, that truth. Such is the case, and importantly so, in Dryden's poetry. When Dryden uses biblical analogy to compare David with Charles or England with Israel, he is not using the biblical term as a signal to be discarded once the contemporary referent has been understood but, rather, invokes both men or both events for the truth that they reveal as part of sacred history. This applies not only to individual images, to the larger biblical vehicle of *Absalom and Achitophel*, but indeed to Dryden's whole shaping of English history as sacred from the Restoration panegyrics to *Britannia Rediviva*. When, in the preface to *Absalom and Achitophel*, he remarks, "Were I the Inventour, who am only the Historian, I should certainly conclude the Piece, with the Reconcilement of *Absalom* to *David*," Dryden is not simply adopting the pose of a naïve scribe, nor is the choice of the biblical narrative simply a convenience for an unresolved situation in Restoration political affairs. Rather, Dryden is stressing the importance as historical truth that both terms (the biblical and the Restoration) share; for, as he shapes the poem, both the biblical and Restoration terms of reference come to embody meanings, by biblical and literary allusion and by typological extension, that are basic to the "truth" of sacred history. Dryden is showing how events in the sacred history of Israel and England recapitulate the basic terms of the Christian paradigm. The Fall at the beginning of human history, the seductive designs of Satan, and the restorative power of God are experiences that all people living under God's covenants share. Read as allegory, *Absalom and Achitophel* is a poem about court intrigue; read with an understanding of the typological significance of biblical narrative, the poem unifies history past and present in an eternal paradigm.

Typology and Analogy

If *allegory* fails as a description of the biblical imagery in Dryden's poetry because it is specific in a wrong way, *analogy* is unsuitable as an account of Dryden's use of biblical characters and events because it is too general a critical term. *Analogy* is misleading, not because it is an incorrect description of the basic operation that links biblical with English history, but because it fails to say what about the analogy between England and Israel is peculiar to sacred history. The analogy between Israel and England, between Noah and Charles, between the murmuring Israelites and the recalcitrant English, is special because it activates the ideas that were commonly associated with the typological interpretation of the Old Testament in the seventeenth century.

The concept of analogy has recently been used as the basis for a lively and judicious study of Dryden's poetry in which the premise is that the "kingdoms" of England, sacred history, and letters serve as interchangeable sources for the ideas and imagery of Dryden's poetry.[59] The virtue of this approach is that it establishes a basic continuity in Dryden's poetic technique and ideas. But the price of this general consistency is a neglect of the equally important distinctions between the quarries to which Dryden went for the materials of his poetry. To take Roman and sacred history as interchangeable quantities is to fail to suggest the different kinds of demands that these histories exert on poetry. To argue that the "function of the biblical fable in *Absalom and Achitophel* is similar to the function of the beast fable in *The Hind and the Panther:* both the kingdom of Jews and the kingdom of beasts will serve to illustrate the kingdom of England" [60] is simply to ignore the kind of pressure that the choice of sacred history as an analogue for English history exerted on Dryden's understanding of the implications of these terms. Moreover, to assign the Restoration panegyrics to the "Kingdom of England" and *Threnodia Augustalis* and *Britannia Rediviva* to the "Kingdom of Adam" is to obscure what the early and late political poems have in common as renderings of England's sacred history. The changing characteristics of biblical imagery in Dryden's political poems have much to tell us both about the individual pieces and about the nature of Dryden's response to the shifting pressures of political life in Restoration England.[61]

Typology, then, in the New Testament is an attempt to see in the narrative history, the personages, and the ceremonies of the Old Testament the permanent figure of the Christian paradigm. In devotional poetry typology extends that paradigm to include the life of the individual believer. In political poetry the typological relationship between past and present invokes for national history and public affairs the same structure of Christian cosmology. Analogy points to a similarity between two events; typology also points to that similarity but locates it as part of an everlasting pattern. To see the historical moment in terms of a typological relationship with the past is to see it as part of that past but also as part of the future. The typological imagery in Dryden's political poetry creates from the particulars of English history an eternal pattern—"The whole Frame render'd was Celestial." [62]

2 THE PRACTICE OF SACRED HISTORIOGRAPHY

Sacred history formed a continuous and well-defined context for political discourse in seventeenth-century England. As a cross section of seventeenth-century materials will illustrate, the use of the England-Israel analogy and the identification of political leaders with biblical patriarchs and kings was a practice limited neither by chronology nor politics. The application of biblical narrative to English history was not the exclusive practice of radical Puritan divines or millenarian prophets during the interregnum years. Rather, as typology was common in both Anglican exegetical tradition and Puritan hermeneutics, so too was the politically informed use of scriptural metaphor and biblical typology in occasional verse, political pamphlets, and sermon literature of the age.[1] The thrust of biblical analogy underwent significant change and intensification during the civil war period, and the intention with which biblical analogy was invoked differed noticeably among the various political groups and at different historical moments. But when Dryden began his career as a political poet in 1659, there was, in the political poetry of his age, a rich variety and well-established tradition of sacred history for him to draw on.[2]

In the general terms of literary history, a shift in sensibility can be clearly located at the turn of the sixteenth century. Gone are the national epic celebrating a virgin queen in the language of classical and national mythology, the intensely petrarchan psychology of the love lyric, and the ebullient comedy of the greenwood. The new age is characterized by the analytical and satiric mood of Donne's *Songs and Sonnets,* the melancholy and introspection of Jacobean drama, and the Anglican scripturalism of Herbert's lyrics. When literary historians consider occasional and political literature at the turn of the century, it is usually to acknowledge the dominantly classical idiom of the Elizabethan masque. Yet literary celebration of the monarch did not simply end with the last book of *The Faerie Queene* or the last graceful exit of Elizabeth as Cynthia from the arcadian woods of the sixteenth-century masque. Political poetry continued to be written, though the swell of lyric and devotional verse of the early seventeenth century has displaced it from critical attention.

It is hardly surprising that readers find Donne and Herbert more compelling than the anonymous or little-known encomiasts and elegists of Elizabeth and her Stuart heirs; yet the displacement of political poetry from critical attention impedes a full understanding of the development of that mode and, consequently, an appreciation of the poetry itself, which, in the years directly preceding and following the Restoration, again came to occupy a position of first importance.[3] Literary historians who find Dryden innovative—or, as recently suggested, working from moribund literary traditions and modes of thought—more often than not reveal uncertainties in their grasp of seventeenth-century literary and intellectual contexts.[4] This was noted long ago with reference to the "originality" of *Absalom and Achitophel*.[5] But Dryden's other political poems also need to be read specifically in the light of their metaphoric settings and the backgrounds against which they were composed.

The dominant note in the literature celebrating Elizabeth is distinctly classical;[6] yet the use of sacred history in commentary on, or celebration of, public figures and events was not, of course, unknown in Elizabethan England. Sermon literature is the obvious respository of examples of biblical narrative used for moral exemplum and historical analogue; but sermon literature in general will not account for the unusual development of political typology in seventeenth-century England. Nor, indeed, does the widespread presence of devotional typology, a characteristic of medieval as well as Renaissance religious expression, suggest any particular reason for the intensified recourse to political typology in the seventeenth century. More significant for this development was the growth of English Puritanism.[7] Under the impetus of Foxe's stories of English martyrs and his interpretation of ecclesiastical and national history, the English Puritans developed a specifically providential and scriptural interpretation of their own fate. The Marian persecution increased the Puritans' conviction that they were indeed the present-day descendants and spiritual heirs of God's favored, yet afflicted, nation.[8] Elizabeth became for her Protestant peoples, though perhaps not by her full consent, a leader of Old Testament cast; and her Protestant enthusiasts spoke of her long reign in the language of scriptural allusion that is so fully developed in later seventeenth-century poetry.[9] Elizabeth was for them Deborah, Judith, or Esther; and England became Israel, Canaan, or Sion.

The Death of Elizabeth

William Leigh's funeral sermons on Elizabeth, together with a funeral elegy on the queen by John Lane, illustrate the intense, significant applications of scriptural narrative to contemporary political affairs at the opening of the century. Leigh's method of paralleling lives and events in Israel and England, and setting such analogies in an explicitly typological paradigm, suggests important trends in Puritan literature of the civil war and interregnum periods. It also provides a useful frame of reference for a poem like *Absalom and Achitophel*, which takes advantage of the identities created by a long tradition of political scripturalism.

The title of Leigh's volume gives a clear indication of his method: *Queene Elizabeth, Paraleld in her Princely vertues, with David, Josua, and Hezekia. 1 With David in her afflictions, to build the Church 2 With Josua in her puissance, to protect the Church 3 With Hezechia in her pietie, to reforme the Church.*[10] The theme of Leigh's first sermon—like afflictions which have followed the godly in all ages—is illustrated by passages on Abraham, Joseph, Moses, Mary, Paul, and Christ. At the beginning of the sermon, Leigh makes explicit the typological relationship that David bears to Christ, and the audience carries the weight of this identification into the David-Elizabeth parallel that closes the sermon. Taking the figure of the ark as a type of God's Church, Leigh expostulates upon "this Arke thus tossed in the deluge, and tyred in the wildernes, despised of the heathen, & much neglected of the true borne Jewe . . . till *David* a *Type* of Christ gave it rest." [11] Toward the end of the sermon Leigh comes to the Davidic parallel, which is of central concern:

Paralell the passions of Princes, Queene *Elizabeth,* with King *Davids* in their grievances, for the maintenance of the religion of their God, and see whether our English *Judah* have not as great cause to pray as ever *Israels Judah* had, *Lord remember Elizabeth in all her afflictions.*

Afflictions, I say afflictions before her raigne, & since her raigne piercing her sacred brest, like a continuall Archers shot, whose arrowes are tipped with gall and sorrow, and now be strong my spirit, & fly out my voyce to compare them in their afflictions.

David was the least and last of his fathers house, so was *Elizabeth* of her fathers familie.

David persecuted from his youth, so was *Elizabeth.*

David contemned of his brethren, *Elizabeth* of her sister, *Saul* a King persecuted *David, Marie* a Queene was wroth with *Elizabeth.*

David an exile in the holdes of *Engeddi,* she close prisoner in the holds of *Wodstocke.*

Doeg reviled *David* unto *Saul,* so did *Gardiner Elizabeth* unto *Mary.*

David declared his innocencie unto *Saul,* so did *Elizabeth* unto her sister, Much was suspected by *David* which they laid unto his charge, things which he never thought, and they ever failed in the proofe.

So was it with *Elizabeth,* her hand yet witnesseth to the innocencie of her soule, which she left as a *constat* of her loyall hart, in these lines, and letters never to be blotted out, *Much suspected by me: nothing proved can be,* quoth *Elizabeth* prisoner.

Saul in his spirit of furie purposed to have killed *David* playing upon his harpe.

Winchester in his spirit of poperie purposed to have murthered *Elizabeth* at her devotions by *Paul Peny* and *James Basset.* . . .

David had many *Doegs* in Court, and *Nabals* in the country, to wrong him with the King, and pinch him in his provision, and not a friend durst speake for him but *Jonathan* . . . shee poore Lady had many Stories in Court to wrong her with the Queene, & to perswade her to strike at the roote, and the branches would wither, many *Nabals* in country, who pined at her provision, and not a *Jonathan* to speake or shoute for her safetie, for that the Queenes heart was implacable.

But see a wonderfull providence of God in her preservation, *Gardiner* hoped to live to see her dead, but she hath lived to see him buried, his flesh turned into dust, and his bones to rottennes.[12]

The weight of the passage is clearly analogical, and the burden of the analogy is easily carried by the many particulars that Leigh cites to support his parallels. In Leigh's sermon the paralleling of David and Elizabeth anticipates certain aspects of the later Puritan manner in sacred historiography; for in Puritan sermons the christological reference often disappears altogether, so that the relationship of Old Testament history to seventeenth-century history can become one of type and antitype. Yet, in this early seventeenth century sermon, the suggestion of the christological center through which the divine runs his parallel histories is still present. If David is a type of Christ in bringing the ark of his Church to rest, so too Elizabeth's afflictions are a shadow of Christ's, "like a continuall Archers shot, whose arrowes are tipped with gall and sorrow." The language, reminiscent of David's (Ps. 69:21), is surely suggestive of the Passion (Matt.

27:34). But the Elizabeth-Christ association is not left at the level of suggestion; at the very close of the sermon Leigh brings it into clear focus: "The allusion is good: from our Christ, to our Queene, for by him and her, the yoke of our burthen, the staffe of our shoulder, and the rodde of our oppressor, hath bene broken, as in the day of *Midian,* and surely till these her *Alcion* dayes, every battel of the warrier hath bin with noise, and tumbling of garments in bloud." [13] As David foreshadowed Christ's role through the afflictions that he suffered "to give the Arke rest," so Elizabeth is a shadow of Christ in the afflictions that she suffered "to build the Church." The assumptions that underlie this passage are important to an understanding of typological thought: David and Elizabeth serve one and the same God; the biblical past and the English present can be easily conflated so that the terms of the analogy are almost interchangeable; and the typological weight of the main characters in the sermon, though it can be obscured by a mass of historical detail, does serve as a basis for the providential nature of the analogy and does clarify the salvific role that both princes play in relation to the chosen people. By casting the terms of English history and the principal actors in Elizabeth's reign into a biblical mold, Leigh is affirming the supposition that the history of God's people as recorded in the Old Testament is repeated again and again in historical time. The language of the Old Testament—as it foreshadows Christ's life and offices, the fate of God's nation, or the terms of Christian eschatology—clarifies and emphasizes the Christian significance of the present moment.[14]

The characteristics of Leigh's first sermon are more pronounced in his second. Elizabeth in the role of protectress of the Church of England takes on not only an ecclesiastical importance but a national one as well. Church and nation are especially close in terms of their common enemies. In the second sermon Leigh arranges the biblical material so that the story of Jacob and Esau serves as an introductory parable to the stories of Joshua in Gibeon and Elizabeth among the Romish Edomites: "Two mightie nations did contend in the

wombe of *Rebecca,* the one is *Esau,* the other is *Jacob.* . . .
Such wofull contentions have ever bin in the wombe of the
Church, betwixt the *Israel* of God, and *Esau* his brood, and
progenie, yet hath not the Lord failed in mercy to deliver his
Turtle-dove from the violence of the assaulter." [15] The Jacob-
Israel-England-Church complex figurally repeats the notion
of God's elect, his "Turtle-dove," his chosen people; while
Esau and, in turn, Ishmael, the Amorites, and the Catholic
Church join hands as enemies of God's elect.

Having established the typological significance of his terms
at the opening of the sermon, Leigh can then trace the pattern
of God's mercy from the record of his people in the Old
Testament to the record of his people in English Judah. The
comparison is not simply analogy but an intensely felt re-
duplication of experience: "As we here find in *Josua* and
feele in our joyfull experience this day." The dynamics of
figural interpretation engages the type at a level of intensity
that changes the simile of analogy into the metaphor of
typology. England is not simply like Israel; it is transformed
into Israel—"the hill of Gods holinesse, *Israel, England,* and
mount *Sion.*" [16] Time and place are collapsed, so that each
component can be shown to share equally in the providential
condition and so that the syntactical juxtaposition can suggest the spiritual and political affinities that Leigh sees in the
relationship between England and Israel.

In devotional typology this bond engages the individual at
the present moment in the eternal drama of salvation. Donne,
preaching on a passage from David's psalms, declares, "But
these *Psalmes* were made, not onely to vent *Davids* present
holy passion, but to serve the Church of God, to the worlds
end. And therefore, change the person, and wee shall finde
a whole quiver of arrows. Extend this *Man,* to all *Mankind;*
carry *Davids* History up to *Adams* History, and consider us in
that state, which wee inherit from *him,* and wee shall see
arrows fly about our ears." [17] In political typology, the emphasis falls not so much on the individual and his relationship
to David's or Adam's history as on the fate and condition of
the whole of God's elect at the present time, and thus on the

relationship between the history of God's chosen people in the Old Testament and the way that God's present elect repeat that history. The Old Testament figures that interested the political poet were therefore often the traditional types for the Church: the ark, the nation of Israelites in exile and redemption, the seed of Abraham; and rather than finding antitypical completion in the person, office, or life of Christ, the Old Testament national political types looked for completion to the Canaan and New Jerusalem of Christian eschatology. In this more traditional use of political typology the land of Canaan in the Old Testament was not a type of present-day England; rather, both Canaan and English Judah were types to be completed at some point in the future.

Along with Leigh's sermons, which it closely resembles, John Lane's funeral elegy on Elizabeth also casts English history into a scriptural mold. England is Israel weeping, Judah forlorn, a barren and overcast Eden; and the queen in her struggle with Spain becomes "*Esther* . . . whose fame (with triumph crownd) / *Haman* of *Spaine* had never force to wound.*"* With Elizabeth's death Spain can triumph: "*Spaine,* clap thy hands, and laugh while we lament, / Our Staffe is broken, and our treasure spent." [18] The elegist uses Scripture in two distinct ways: first, in a generalized association of common biblical terms with the English and England (the English as Jacob's seed and the "litle flock"; England as Israel, Sion, Judah, and Canaan); second, in a more specific application of a particular biblical narrative to a particular political situation. The generalized application of biblical terms had considerable typological weight; the typology of Canaan and Eden was accessible and commonplace during the period. In the second instance, the application of the story of Esther to the fate of Elizabeth and the English at the hands of a Spanish Haman was undoubtedly a contemporary invention (but not necessarily an invention of the elegist). Although the exaltation of Esther before Ahasuerus was often understood as prefiguring the Assumption of the Virgin, in this instance the figural power of Esther's story depends on the context that the elegist supplies. Out of context the analogy between Elizabeth and Esther or between Philip and Haman need not carry special meaning; but within the scriptural frame it becomes part of the typological repetition of the story of God's elect. Once the identification of England with Israel is set in motion, the salvation of the Israelites through Esther's intervention with Ahasuerus becomes a suitable parable for a scriptural reading of Elizabeth's resistance to Spanish pressures. As in so many instances, then, the poem as a whole determines the meaning of individual pieces of biblical narrative. Rather than expecting specific verbal signals to accompany each text, one must learn to use the context that the poet or divine provides in determining whether the typological meaning is being invoked and to what extent typology completes or enhances the structure and meaning of the passage in question.

The Reigns of the First Stuarts

Conforming to the formulaic cry "The king is dead, long live the king," John Lane's elegy on Elizabeth concludes with a greeting to the new monarch: "Chaunt loud *Poeanas* to his loftie Fame, / And songs of praise to high *Jehovas* Name." [19] Drawing on New as well as Old Testament material, the elegist uses imagery from Revelation to cast James's role in the struggle against Spain in apocalyptic terms: "Laugh not (proud *Spaine*) nor lift not up thy crest, / But hide thy horns thou seven headed beast." In the remainder of the passage, England is identified with Israel, the monarch sits on David's throne, and one and the same God who watched over the Old Testament elect still keeps "his litle flock." The assumptions that explain the relevance and logic of analogizing Elizabeth with figures such as David, Joshua, Esther, and Deborah also explain James's presence in the elegy as Gideon and as a Davidic king.

The Old Testament type who was most frequently used for James, however, was not David, but Solomon. It is not difficult to understand why the king's contemporaries felt that

Solomon was the most appropriate correlative type for James I. Perhaps incompetent in matters of political compromise, nevertheless James was learned in questions of theology and church government, and no less a scholar than John Donne invoked Solomon in his sermon on the death of the king. Though not partisan in application, this sermon, on the Song of Solomon 3:11, is worth considering for the manner in which Donne handles the typology of Solomon, Christ, and James I.[20] The persons in the text are identified as the speaker (the Church, the Spouse of Christ), the persons that are called up (the Daughters of Sion), and the person to whom the words of the text are addressed ("*Solomon* crowned, That is, Christ invested with the royall dignity of being *Head of the Church*" [21]). The typology is traditional, as is the allegorical context in which it is set. Of particular interest, however, is Donne's inclusion of James I in the typological paradigm:

> Here, at your coming hither now, you have *two glasses,* wherein you may see your selves from head to foot; One in the Text, your *Head, Christ Jesus,* represented unto you, in the name and person of *Solomon, Behold King Solomon crowned, &c.* And another, under your feet, in the dissolution of this great *Monarch,* our *Royall Master,* now layd lower by death then any of us, his Subjects and servants.[22]

Christ in the figure of Solomon is one glass; James, "this great *Monarch,* our *Royall Master,*" is the other. The relationship between the two glasses is more than adventitious: Solomon prefigures Christ, James is Christ's shadow. The intention of the sermon is not to enhance the king or deflate his enemies but, as is usual with Donne, to involve the audience deeply and persuasively in the Christian paradigm. Salvation, not politics, was Donne's concern in both the devotional poems and the sermons, and he addressed his work to the Christian audience and to himself as Christian speaker.

Quite different in tone from Donne's sermon, though relying on the same complex of interpretive ideas, is Herrick's *Pastorall upon the birth of Prince Charles, Presented to the*

King, and Set by Mr. Nic: Laniere. The rustic conversation between the shepherds borrows the language and strategy of the conventional nativity piece. The scene recalls the medieval *pastores* and suggests, in a modest way, the opening of Milton's *On the Morning of Christ's Nativity:*

> *Mirt.* And that his birth sho'd be more singular,
> At Noone of Day, was seene a silver Star,
> Bright as the Wise-mens Torch, which guided them
> To Gods sweet Babe, when borne at *Bethlehem;*
> While Golden Angels (some have told to me)
> Sung out his Birth with Heav'nly Minstralsie.
> *Amint.* O rare! But is't a trespasse if we three
> Sho'd wend along his Baby-ship to see?
> *Mirt.* Not so, not so. *Chor.* But if it chance to prove
> At most a fault, 'tis but a fault of love.
> *Amar.* But deare *Mirtillo,* I have heard it told,
> Those learned men brought *Incense, Myrrhe,* and *Gold,*
> From Countries far, with store of Spices, (sweet)
> And laid them downe for Offrings at his feet.
> *Mirt.* 'Tis true indeed; and each of us will bring
> Unto our smiling, and our blooming King,
> A neat, though not so great an Offering.
> *Amar.* A Garland for my Gift shall be
> Of flowers, ne'r suckt by th'theeving Bee:
> And all most sweet; yet all lesse sweet than he.
> *Amint.* And I will bear along with you
> Leaves dropping downe the honyed dew,
> With oaten pipes, as sweet, as new.
> *Mirt.* And I a Sheep-hook will bestow,
> To have his little King-ship know,
> As he is Prince, he's Shepherd too.[23]

Charles as prince and shepherd, the eastern star, the gifts—the identification of Charles with Christ is unmistakable. Jonson said of Donne's *Anniversarie* that "if it had been written of ye Virgin Marie it had been something," and one wonders what he thought of Herrick's conflation of Charles with Christ, of the linking of the two nativity scenes. Yet the identification of a king or prince with Christ was common and depended on a well-established understanding of the relationship between Old Testament, New Testament, and contemporary figures.

The Civil War and the Interregnum

Herrick's delicate Royalist encomium on the future Charles II is remote from the imagery of deluge and martyrdom that characterizes the literature on Charles I's execution; yet in time it is less than twenty years away. The execution of the king, however, did not shatter the biblical context in which a poem like Herrick's *Pastorall* is set and in which the Royalists saw the divinely anointed carrying out God's tasks. The Royalists simply reassessed the situation and returned to the Bible to seek new texts with which to explain present circumstances or new ways in which to interpret already familiar Scripture. Nor were the Puritan defenders of the Commonwealth slow to adapt Scripture to their political purposes or to develop a distinctive scriptural rhetoric and point of view.

At the opening of the century Protestant voices united in lamenting English Judah's loss of her queen and in chanting hosannas for the new occupant of David's throne. But by the time of the civil war, and for the next twenty years, the split in political thinking was forcefully echoed in the literature celebrating or defending Royalist and Parliamentarian causes. In the Royalist elegies for Charles I the king came to seem increasingly, perhaps alarmingly, like Christ in the Passion. The Royalists emphasized the typology of kingship—sacrificial imagery and the language of sacred anointment. For the king's party the complex of typological associations that looked back to the Edenic state and forward to the New Jerusalem no longer seemed relevant. Indeed, in some of the funeral pieces for Charles I, England was transformed into a blighted Egypt or Sodom.[24] In Puritan literature, however, examples from sacred history were marshaled to defend past and present political action and the theme of an imminent Sion became increasingly popular.

THE PURITAN OFFENSIVE

Milton, one of many Puritan writers on political questions, argued vigorously from scriptural example against the divine nature of temporal kingship. He sought evidence in the Old Testament to support his view that the Commonwealth was the form of government that God favored for the Israelite nation and declared by scriptural authority that God preferred judges to kings.[25] In *A Defence of the People of England* (1651), answering the assertion of Salmasius that kings are of God and therefore must not be resisted, Milton challenged his opponent by turning to the example of Rehoboam in 1 Kings: "I assert that by God's testimony popular assemblies, elections, campaigns, votes and enactments are equally of God. . . . so it is certain that today free popular assemblies are of God and may therefore compel the compliance of their kings or cast them off." [26]

But neither Milton nor his political allies and contemporaries limited their use of Scripture simply to justifying a particular act by the sanction of scriptural authority. Like Calvin, who in the *Institutes* found that the political example of biblical judges was a pattern to be observed in forming a constitution for church and state, Milton favored a government for England patterned on the example of Mosaic theocracy.[27] In *The Tenure of Kings and Magistrates* Milton argued that as God was angry with the Israelites when they rejected him and his form of government for a king, so will he "bless us, and be propitious to us who reject a King to make him onely our leader and supreme governour in the conformity as neer as may be of his own ancient government." [28] God's mutual election of England and Israel formed the premise of Milton's scriptural polemics. "Why else," Milton had asked in *Areopagitica,* "was this Nation chos'n before any other, that out of her as out of *Sion* should be proclaim'd and sounded forth the first tidings and trumpet of Reformation to all *Europ?*" [29]

Finding scriptural models for the interregnum government characterizes a development in Puritan typology in which England was transformed from simply a type of the elect people into the antitype, the fulfillment of God's first elect nation. The New Sion that Puritan preachers saw in the not distant future of English history became the antitype of the Old Testament Sion; and the redemptive history of Israel, rather than prefiguring some distant state in the corporate history of the elect or some personal condition in the after-life of the blessed, was thought to prefigure England's immediate deliverance by Parliament.

For some the familiar Exodus motif foreshadowed Parliament's leading the Israelites out of the wilderness of Antichrist; for others Parliament was the antitype of Joseph as shepherd of Israel; and for still others it was the antitype of Solomon's temple.[30] These individual readings are often interesting for their ingenuity, but the whole tendency to transform the relationship of England and Israel into type and antitype is a more important characteristic of Puritan uses of sacred history. With the transformation of England from type to antitype came a transformation in Puritan exegetical writing. As the antitype shifted from a christological or eschatological center to a current or imminent historical point, the typological relationship between past and present changed, so that, in the more radical Puritan writers, the Old Testament events tended to lose their historical significance and become signs, keys, or mirrors by which to read the importance of the present event. The "lively Parallels" of Henry Dawbeny's *Historie and Policie Re-viewed* suggest the direction that Puritan sacred historiography took: "I believe, truly, that there is no intelligent Person living, that looks upon this Story, of our present Ascent, but would take the particulars of the children of Israels Deliverance, to be throughout Typical of ours, and all the circumstances of effecting it by the first *Moses,* as plainly to apply themselves, to our glorious second [Cromwell]." [31]

As the Puritan exegetes focused more intensely on the antitype of the immediate present, the past lost its historicity and the "Perfect Register" of the Holy Scripture became, in the words of the Puritan divine Robert Baillie, a glass wherein "we may behold the cleare Image of our dayes." The focus of Baillie's typology is the immediate problem of overcoming the obstacles that lay in the path of effecting the New Jerusalem; as Baillie asked, "In the midst of so huge difficulties as this day on all sides beset us, how shall our Sion be gotten builded?" [32]

As the identification of England with Israel intensified or changed, so that Israel became a type of the antitypical England, the millenarian strain in Puritan exegetical writing echoed the general emphasis on the present and immediate future as the stage of God's revelatory work. Relying on contemporary astrology and drawing on various traditions of sacred numerology and biblical interpretation, including cabalistic methods of searching Scripture, the more confirmed prophets were busy during the interregnum years calculating and revising their predictions for the coming of the millennium. The more extreme aspects of Puritan scripturalism have no great importance in themselves for the background of Dryden's writing, but they indicate dramatically the tendency in Puritan thought to treat Scripture as hidden agenda. Biblical typology in general provides a structure in which two poles of history take meaning from each other; with typological analogy the correlative terms are related to each other and to a third term. In the more radical Puritan writers, the emphasis on the present as the focus of the past could reduce the past to a position of secondary importance similar to that of Old Testament figures and events in the medieval type-antitype relationship.

The radical exegetes' prophetical keys, numerical calculations, and schematizations of Old Testament history form part of the Puritan tradition in biblical study, but they do not represent the whole.[33] The numerous typology manuals published in the 1640s and 1650s illustrate some of the same drive toward schematization, but in general their focus is more purely scriptural. Their roots are much deeper in the central exegetical tradition and their influence in post-Restoration culture much more pervasive than the millenarian studies in prophetic numerology or legal astrology. Rather than theological treatises, works like Taylor's *Moses and Aaron*, Guild's *Moses unveiled*, and Mather's *Figures or Types* are compendiums of scriptural commentary. Meant for popular use, they made available in abundant detail typological expositions of the Old Testament prophets, kings, events, and ceremonies. That these commentaries had become common by mid-century and that their general influence persisted through the end of the century is confirmed both by the number of manuals produced and by their frequent reprintings. They undoubtedly played a significant role in giving currency to the vocabulary of types and to an interpretation of the prominent Old Testament figures and events that had always been a part of biblical commentary. Indeed, the pulpit and press in Dryden's age were saturated with the vocabulary of types, and the original England-Israel metaphor was intensified and extended to accommodate such subtle varieties of meaning as those found in *Absalom and Achitophel*.

THE ROYALIST DEFENSE

The Puritan emphasis on typology in general and on the political implications of Old Testament history is part of the background of Dryden's poetry. But Anglican-Royalist literature and its recourse to the typology of kingship is also an important, and even more obvious, component of Dryden's handling of sacred history. The comparisons of Charles II to biblical figures that are found in Restoration panegyrics and continued in satires and later occasional poems can be understood in terms of the typology of kingship and are directly indebted to the tradition of kingly types.

A good introduction to the material on Charles I is *Mercurius Davidicus, or a Patterne of loyall Devotion*, published in 1643, well before the outcome of the civil war had been decided. This pamphlet consists of a series of prayers asking the Lord of Hosts to take a firm stand against his enemies and the enemies of his anointed. Its language suggests several associations that can be found in Royalist literature well through the Restoration. Calling on the Lord of Hosts to destroy the anointed king's enemies, the anonymous author exclaims,

> Make them like a fiery oven in the time of thy wrath; destroy them in thy displeasure: Root out their fruit from the earth, and their seed from among the children of men, because they have intended mischief against thine Anointed *Charles,* and imagined such a devise, which wee beseech thee they may not be able to performe. . . .
>
> Break the hornes of the ungodly people; and at thy rebuke, let both the Horse and his Charriot fall; That thy servant *David,* and our Soveraigne *Charles,* may againe feed us with a faithfull and true heart, & rule us prudently with all his power. . . .
>
> . . . Thou hast made a covenant with thy chosen, thou hast sworn unto *David* (unto *Charles*) thy servant; O doe thou establish his seed for ever & set up his throne from one generation to another; Thou hast Anointed him with thy holy Oile, now let thy Hand hold him fast, and thine Arm strengthen him; That the enemie may not be able to doe him violence, nor these sonnes of wickednesse to hurt him; Smite down his foes before his face, and plague them that hate him. . . .
>
> . . . Lord, remember this *David* of thine, and all his troubles; and turne not away the presence of thine Anointed; Clothe his enemies with shame, but upon himself let his Crown flourish.[34]

Directions on the title page of *Mercurius Davidicus* indicate that it was suitable for use by the king's army before and after battle, which, no doubt, accounts for its strident tone. But besides applying Old Testament formulas to contemporary public prayer, it repeatedly refers to Charles and David as God's anointed, intensifying their relationship at each rhetorical step: first, "thy servant *David,* and our Soveraigne *Charles*"; then, "unto *David* (unto *Charles*)"; and finally, "this *David* of thine."

The twin theme of Davidic kingship and sacred anointment figured importantly in Royalist literature before the
civil war and after the Restoration; indeed, the theme of
Davidic kingship had special meaning in both Puritan-Parliamentarian and Royalist apologetics. For Puritan writers,
David of the Psalms personified the holy and true ministry; [35]
but it was for the king's party that David of the Old Testament historical books came to symbolize royal stature in civil
and ecclesiastical matters. Dryden, for one, used the Davidic
parallel or allusion in all three of his Restoration poems. In
Mercurius Davidicus Charles as Davidic king repeats David's
covenanted relationship with God and recalls the troubled
times of the biblical king. Though there is still in 1643 reference to the king's party as divinely chosen, the emphasis is on
the beleaguered state of this present-day biblical monarch.
After the execution of Charles I, the theme of Davidic kingship in Royalist literature was superseded by the language of
sacrificial kingship; but with the Restoration there was a
strong resurgence of the Davidic theme.[36]

The sacred anointment of kings is the second important
theme in *Mercurius Davidicus*. The favor that this theme
found in Royalist literature is explained by a work like Richard Mocket's *God and the King*. A Royalist apologia first
published under James I, it went through several editions
after the Restoration and can thus be regarded as representative Royalist propaganda. Addressing himself to the question
of the source of the king's authority, Mocket asks:

> For from whence have they received their Soveraignty
> to be here upon earth as gods over men? God himself an-
> swereth, [Psal. 82.] *I* (and not any creature whatsoever)
> *have said, ye are Gods:* and as by my Word the world
> was made; so are ye appointed by the same Word to rule
> the world. . . . Neither the kingdom only, and the power
> of Princes, but all these things else proper unto them,
> are after a peculiar manner Gods. Their [Psal. 21.]
> *Crown,* their [Psal. 89.] *Anointing,* their [2 Chron. 9.]
> *Scepter* and *Throne* are Gods; and their persons, adorned
> with all these, are so Divine and Sacred, that they them-

selves are the [2 Sam. 14.] *Angels of God,* and [Psal. 82.] *sons of the most High.*[37]

Sacred anointment is a symbol of divinely invested royal authority. Along with the two other royal symbols of scepter and throne, it crystallized the divine analogy and became a powerful weapon for the monarchy in the legal and political dialectic of the age.[38] Sacred anointment, as the language of Mocket's argument illustrates, firmly established the king's position in relation to his biblical precedents and reaffirmed the paradigm of typology: as the biblical kings of the Old Testament were consecrated in their kingly office (e.g., 1 Sam. 9:16), as Christ was anointed with the Holy Ghost (Luke 4:18 or Acts 4:27, 10:38), so the English king was anointed in his office. The twin theme of sacred anointment and biblical kingship is prominent in the coronation ceremony of Charles II, in which the ritual of sacred anointment—"Let these hands be anointed with the Holy Oyl, as Kings and Prophets have been anointed"—is followed by the anthem—"*Sadoc* the Priest and *Nathan* the Prophet anointed *Solomon* King, and all the People rejoyced, and said, *God save the King.*" [39]

The language and strategy of divine kingship continued to exert a powerful influence on Royalist literature throughout the civil war period. In *The Kings Disguise,* Cleveland makes specific application of figural imagery in commenting on the proper glory of the kingly office and the present shame that the person of Charles I endured:

> But pardon Sir, since I presume to be
> Clarke of this Closet to Your Majestie;
> Me thinks in this your dark mysterious dresse
> I see the Gospell coucht in Parables.
> The second view my pur-blind fancy wipes,
> And shewes Religion in its dusky types.
> Such a Text Royall, so obscure a shade
> Was *Solomon* in Proverbs all array'd.[40]

Assuming the role of royal confessor, Cleveland interprets the meaning of the king's mysterious dress in a threefold analogy

based on the language of scriptural interpretation. The king
is in turn compared to three scriptural types; and by terms of
the last analogy both Solomon and Charles are types of Christ
the King.[41] The mechanics of the typological analogy are in-
tricate, but the idea itself was commonplace.

The conclusion of the poem intensifies the use of Old
Testament analogy:

> Mount then thou shadow royall, and with haste
> Advance thy morning star, *Charles*'s overcast.
> May thy strange journey contradictions twist,
> And force faire weather from a Scottish mist.
> Heavens Confessors are pos'd, those star-ey'd Sages,
> To interpret an Ecclipse thus riding stages.
> Thus *Israel*-like he travells with a cloud,
> Both as a Conduct to him, and a shroud.
> But oh! he goes to *Gibeon,* and renewes
> A league with mouldy bread, and clouted shooes.[42]

The passage opens with a play on the natural and scriptural
meaning of *shadow*. In his physical disguise the king is in
eclipse, but the phrase "shadow royall" also picks up the
earlier reference to Solomon as a "Text Royall." This scriptural meaning of *shadow* is then extended in line 121, where
the king's flight from his pursuers is compared to the Israelites' exodus from Egypt and flight across the desert. The
whole Exodus story is, of course, weighted with typological
significance, but the analogy between the king's escape and
the scriptural Exodus is an inversion both of the literal story
of the Israelites' flight toward Canaan and of the typological
interpretation of the Exodus as a figure of salvation. The
king's flight ends not in literal or figural salvation but in a
league with the Scots (the "mouldy bread, and clouted
shooes" of line 124).

Against the Exodus passage Cleveland plays another biblical
episode. The reference in the last couplet is to the story from
Joshua 9 in which the Israelites are tricked into a false league
with disguised Gibeonites. This juxtaposition of biblical episodes as a narrative device not only contrasts the present-day

event with past events but also permits the biblical episodes to serve as commentaries on each other; it is a device that Dryden frequently uses. The theme of providential disguise is given a perplexing variety of treatments in Cleveland's poem; with the aid of various metaphorical devices, not the least important of which is the typological analogy, Cleveland manages to inspect his theme from several points of view. The poet's hope for, yet irritation with, the king is filtered through the language of scriptural reference. We are on the one hand commanded to regard the king's disguise as libelous and archaic; yet to describe the king Cleveland also chooses biblical metaphors with positive connotations. It has been argued that this conflation of attitudes, so far from sanctifying monarchy, only makes religion seem quaint,[43] but the scriptural and Christian significance of the kingly office may not reduce so easily. The biblical imagery in Cleveland's other poems—for example, *The Mixt Assembly, The Rebell Scot,* and *Upon the Kings return from Scotland*—suggests that he was sharply aware of the serious as well as ironic potential of typological imagery. Scriptural metaphor in *The Kings Disguise* supports the sanctity of the monarch; it does not collapse under the weight of those passages in which Cleveland castigates the person of the king.

CHARLES I'S EXECUTION

From the time of the king's flight to the Scots until his execution on 30 January 1649, less than two years elapsed. But with the execution an important change took place in the iconography of Charles I. If in late 1646 or early 1647 Cleveland still thought it proper to assume the tone of a scourge in the king's defense, by the time of the first elegies on the king's death Charles I had been transformed into a perfect martyr—indeed, into Christ in the Passion. The use of biblical iconography in the elegiac material on Charles I is an important development in Royalist applications of sacred history and extends the range of biblical reference available for the Royalist propaganda arsenal after the Restoration.[44]

An anonymous broadside on the king's death turns to biblical analogy as a simple device to heighten the personal attractiveness of the "butcher'd Martyr King" and "persecuted Saint":

> Patient as *Job,* and like to *Moses,* milde,
> *Salomons* wisedome makes him Wisedomes childe;
> Valient as *David,* and the chiefest part
> Like to *Josiah,* zeale possest his heart:
> Faithfull in Vowes, yet there began the strife,
> That reav'd him of his *Queene,* his *Crowne,* his *Life:*
> Whose true Effigies drawne by just desert,
> Causeth him live in each true Subjects heart:
> Living he dy'd, and dying life he gain'd,
> Death conquer'd him, his foes with shame he stain'd.[45]

These comparisons stress attributes of character rather than similarities of office or historical circumstance. Thus the dynamics of biblical analogy do not reach beyond the individual comparison to become a structural principle. A substitution of classical worthies would not make a fundamental difference to the procedure of the poem. That is not the case with typological analogy, in which correspondence between Old Testament and contemporary figures depends explicitly or implicitly on the relationship of both halves of the analogy to a third term, the antitype of biblical typology. In correlative typology, the contemporary figure is a shadow of the christological antitype, looking backward in time to its fulfillment or forward to the eschaton. In the elegies and commemorative verse on the king's execution the most prominent typological relationship takes the king as a shadow of the christological antitype.

An anonymous elegy in the collection *Monumentum Regale* (1649) states explicitly the Charles-Christ typology:

> Now *Charles* as *King,* and as a *good King too,*
> Being *Christs adopted self,* was both to do
> And *suffer* like him; both to live and die
> So much more *humble,* as he was more *high*

> Then his own *Subjects.* He was thus to tread
> In the same footsteps, and submit his Head
> To the same *thorns,* when *spit* upon, and *beat,*
> To make his *Consciences* serve for his *retreat,*
> And *overcome* by *suffering:* To take up
> His Saviours *Crosse,* and pledge him in his *Cup.*[46]

The mechanics of the analogy in the first two lines are those that Dryden used in *Threnodia Augustalis,* making Charles "That all forgiving King, / The type of him above" (ll. 257–58). Similarly, they represent the very assumption on which medieval political theology relied in postulating the christo-mimetic identity of the Christian king. In the medieval cathedral, sculptural programs and stained glass windows that alluded to the typological relationship of Old Testament and medieval rulers relied on the same assumptions that are at the base of political typology in the seventeenth century.[47] The continuity of biblical imagery from the medieval sculptural program to the Renaissance coronation ode affirms the central importance of the figural interpretation of sacred history and its continuing relevance to public life through the Renaissance to the end of the seventeenth century. The language of types was one that the designers of stained glass windows at Chartres shared with Marvell and Dryden. The link between these two points in history is not, of course, one particular interpretive text but a tradition of biblical interpretation practiced by the Latin church fathers, circumscribed but reaffirmed by Reformation commentary, and echoed and schematized in the typology manuals of the seventeenth century.

The typology of kingship and the analogy with Christ are part of a well-defined tradition of typological thought. The specific motif of Charles I as "Christ's adopted self" recurs frequently in the elegiac material and is part of the language used to celebrate Charles II at the Restoration; what is unusual, though obviously a product of historical circumstance, is the development of the analogy between the Passion and Charles I's execution. The elegy from *Monumentum Regale* proceeds directly from the typology of Charles and Christ to the analogy: "He was thus to tread / In the same footsteps, and submit his Head / To the same *thorns.*" Similarly, in John Warner's *Devilish Conspiracy* the identification of Charles with Christ is collapsed into "King Ch.," and the ambiguity of the phrase "anointed of the Lord" is played on in order to develop a typological relationship between Charles and Christ as the basis for a sermon against the king's Puritan executioners as Jews.[48] The backdrop of the Crucifixion be-became a familiar scene in the poems commemorating the king's execution.[49] The Crucifixion was read as double history, and the identification of it with the king's execution was based on the assumption that the king was, at least in the language of political theology, Christ's adopted self.

Out of the analogy between the Crucifixion and Charles's execution—between the Jews and the Puritans—developed an interesting alternate potential of Israelite history. The challenge of the Puritan insistence on their identity as the elect nation was taken up by Royalist literature; defenders of the crown were not slack in recognizing more than one possibility latent in the meaning of Old Testament narrative. If Puritan literature proposed that Cromwell-Moses was leading the elect nation toward the New Jerusalem, the Royalist Henry King, lamenting the king's execution, could ask, "But what! could Israel find no other way / To their wish'd Canaan than through This Red Sea?"[50] King, in his funeral elegy, turns the language of Puritan election back on the political acts of the king's enemies; the biblical metaphor is shown to have an application to the king's cause as well as to that of Puritan poets and divines. The Red Sea as the king's blood is a two-way metaphor in King's elegy that had considerable attraction for Royalist defenders. Another anonymous elegy from *Monumentum Regale* offers an interesting variation on that metaphor. It first states the typological basis of the analogy between Charles and Christ: "Where my *Faith* resting on th'*Originall*, / Supports it self in this the *Copies* fall."[51] The terms are variations on the more familiar type and antitype, shadow and fulfillment. In the next few lines the *"Red floud"* of Charles I's blood is identified with the *"Bloody wood"* of the cross, and finally the Red Sea is associated with the deluge and destruction visited on the Egyptians. A complex of familiar images is called up in this Royalist application of Exodus material.

The Royalist elegies for Charles I, with their strong emphasis on the typology of kingship, have an important relationship to Restoration poetry in general and Dryden's contribution to that literature in particular. But as important as the emphasis on the relationship between king and Christ is the doubling of terms from Jewish history; for, by the time of the Restoration, the intense, almost frenetic, expression of biblical identity in the writings of Puritan divines and millenarian prophets had firmly identified the Puritan-Parliamentarian cause with the elect nation of Old Testament history. The elegies and sermons on Charles I that begin by conflating his execution and the Crucifixion, and develop by way of analogy between the Jews and the Parliamentarians, are taking advantage of a ready-made identification. No one had insisted on the identification of Old Testament history with Parliamentarian history more than the Puritans. But Royalist elegies on Charles I—and, in turn, Royalist apologetics transformed into such art as *Absalom and Achitophel*—brought this identification to a new completeness. The Israelites were guided toward Canaan by the pillar and the cloud, but they also murmured in the desert, and Dryden was not reluctant to use both sides of this piece of providential history. If Charles was alternately Noah and David to the English Israelites, Dryden also gives ample scope to a portrait of that elect nation in *Absalom and Achitophel:*

> The *Jews,* a Headstrong, Moody, Murmuring race,
> As ever try'd th'extent and stretch of grace;
> God's pamper'd people whom, debauch'd with ease,
> No King could govern, nor no God could please.
>
> [45–48]

The flexibility and the resilience of the metaphor, its power both to sanctify and to deflate, was the result of a long tradition of figural reading and a fervently topical, contemporary exploration of the relevance of Scripture to English history. The foundation of biblical metaphor in political literature of the seventeenth century was typology, but the full potential of this source of metaphorical history was realized in the variety of seventeenth-century applications of Old Testament narrative. Anglican and Puritan exegetical thought, Royalist and Parliamentarian political theory—all shaped the meaning of biblical history for seventeenth-century England. At times Dryden's use of Old Testament history reveals the specifically typological nature of the analogy between Old Testament and seventeenth-century event, but in many cases the typological basis is not specifically cited. The strength of this metaphoric construct can be found in the long tradition that defines and sanctifies the relationship between the Old Testament and the New, between the history of God's chosen people before the Incarnation and the history of that nation after the New Dispensation.

MARVELL's *First Anniversary*

Before *Absalom and Achitophel, The First Anniversary* is perhaps the most significant political poem to use figural imagery. It was probably an important precedent for Dryden, but clearly no specific precedent was necessary to activate or justify the political application of typology.

It has been argued that Marvell portrays Cromwell as an instrument of Providence and a principle of order and that Marvell accomplishes this, in part, by drawing on a field of biblical imagery and on specific biblical characters who carry figural weight.[52] Thus the Davidic king was the most important of the types, subsuming or integrating much of the classical and biblical imagery, and having a specifically political significance. The Davidic figure combined authority and kingship with the image of the humble psalmist, which in turn carried suggestions of cosmic harmony. From this double association, it is argued, Marvell presents a portrait of Cromwell in which the twin aspects of the Davidic king—harmony and authority—are combined. However, this argument, based exclusively on medieval typology, neglects or underestimates the significance of some of the biblical material in the poem that does not so easily assimilate with the Davidic *figura* but that can be explained by typological tradition contemporary with Marvell.[53] The picture of Cromwell as Moses leading the Israelites toward a very imminent New Jerusalem and the use of imagery from Revelation and the prophetic books of the Old Testament were important elements in Puritan literature during the interregnum years.

To emphasize the medieval concept of the Davidic king is to neglect Marvell's reference to Gideon and biblical judgeship:

> When *Gideon* so did from the War retreat,
> Yet by the Conquest of two Kings grown great,
> He on the Peace extends a Warlike power,
> And *Is'rel* silent saw him rase the Tow'r;
> And how he *Succoths* Elders durst suppress,
> With Thorns and Briars of the Wilderness.
> No King might ever such a Force have done;
> Yet would not he be Lord, nor yet his Son.[54]

Cromwell as a correlative of Gideon is here a significant element in the portrait and cannot be explained simply as a reference to Cromwell's refusal to accept the crown. For the Puritan exegetes, Gideon, like Samson, was not to be fulfilled in the antitype of Christ the king but in the antitype of Christ the judge. The Old Testament judges were interpreted in Protestant scriptural commentary as figures chosen by God "to defend and deliver the people from their oppressors, and to re-establish the publike liberty and peace by their Armies, miraculously conducted and blessed by God." [55] The pattern of biblical judgeship does much to shape the meaning of Cromwell in *The First Anniversary,* as does the antitypical completion of the Old Testament figure in the apocalyptic material of the New Testament. Marvell's inclusion of the Gideon reference creates a more complex figural nature for Cromwell: the theme of biblical judgeship is not simply to be collapsed into the motif of Davidic kingship. Perhaps, as with the disparate elements in Marvell's *Horatian Ode* (1650), the various scriptural motifs are to be held in a tension that shapes the poem as a whole.

The Restoration and After

The ambiguity that Marvell preferred, Restoration panegyrists found less congenial. For most, the Restoration was a welcome event, and the panegyrical and commendatory verse, as well as the records of contemporary historians, reflect the general enthusiasm that greeted the king on his return. The accounts of Clarendon, Parker, Pepys, Burnet, and Evelyn give credence to lines 21–28 in *Astraea Redux,* which register the strain of the interregnum years.[56] But neither *Astraea Redux* nor the other panegyrical verse written on the Restoration are circumscribed by the language of contemporary events. The king's encomiasts, as might be expected, turned to classical and sacred history for terms of praise and heroic analogues. Yet the treatment of biblical history in these poems is not adequately described as historical allusion. The seventeenth-century understanding of Old Testament narrative included, at least in part, the typological reading of Old Testament figure and event, and this figural perspective was clearly an important element in much of the occasional verse and politically minded sermons of the Restoration era. To suppose that that age was somehow cut off from this biblical tradition —to hypothesize that Dryden was not alive to the general stream of biblical interpretation that informed *Paradise Lost* [57] —is to ignore a large body of evidence to the contrary.

Edward Boteler's sermon *Jus Poli et Fori: or, God and the King* (delivered in 1660) makes a good introduction to Restoration sermons and panegyrics because Boteler so clearly states the typological basis of his application of biblical history to contemporary events.[58] The sermon, preached on Psalm 72:4, begins by invoking the familiar parallel between the Israelites and the English, but here the analogy is between the captive Jews of Babylon and the presumably loyal Englishmen of the interregnum. Within this general context Boteler sets his reading of the psalm: "I know, a greater then *Solomon* is here, but yet *Solomon* is here too; *Solomon* in the figure, and Christ in the perfection of Kingly administration." [59] He explicitly rejects the interpretation of exegetes who made Solomon only an appellative for Christ. Rather, he reads "*Solomon* in the figure" and "Christ in the perfection" —the terms of traditional biblical typology. Boteler's reading conforms to Augustine's insistence on the truth of sacred history, which can be read profitably in itself and even more profitably in spiritual (typological) terms.[60] This interpretation of Solomon and Christ depends, as well, on the mutual historicity of the two events in a figural relationship.[61] Expounding on the office of Christ as king, Boteler writes, "This is He, the first He, He in the Antitype, and by way of Eminency. *He shall judge the poor of the people.*" He then turns from Christ as king to Charles as king:

> Here is an He in the Type too, another He, deputed, authorized, commissioned from Heaven, and instructed with the management of judgement till that day, and *He also shall judge the poore of the people.*
>
> And if you aske who he is, though the matchless iniquity of the late times interdicted all mention of him with that honour due unto his Name, forcing men either to cancell or conceale it, and pouring contempt upon it: yet blessed be God, we may now speake out! this He is the King. *He shall judge the, &c.*[62]

The typological center of the analogy between Solomon and Charles and the dynamics of typological kingship could hardly be stated with greater clarity. Boteler's sermon tries to make whole once again the identity of both king and people in terms of a typological relationship with the nation and kings of Old Testament Israel.

The uniting of nation and king through biblical analogy and biblical typology marks a number of other sermons, panegyrics, and miscellaneous items occasioned by the Restoration.[63] In 1661 Thomas Pierce, for example, reminded his audience of their late Egyptian bondage in *A Sermon preached on the 29th day of May*. In reviewing the parallel histories of God's nation of Israelites and his present people, Pierce makes their typological relationship very clear. Having dwelt on the hardships and rewards that God alternately dealt his Old Testament nation, Pierce then turns to the present day:

> Passe we now (if you please) out of the *Vineyard* into the *Fold;* from the *People* under the *Law,* to *Us* who live under the *Gospel;* whom though our Lord (out of *goodness*) was pleas'd to call his *Flock of Sheep,* he might have stil'd (out of *Justice*) his *Herd of Swine.* . . . And this may point us out a *Reason,* why for so *many years together,* (before this *last,*) our heavenly Father made use of his *sharpest Methods* for our *amendment;* even placing us as *Israelites* amongst *Egyptians.*[64]

The typological base of the analogy between God's two elect nations is evident in the language with which Pierce begins the present-day half of the analogy, passing from the people under the Law to the people under the Gospel. But national election is not Pierce's only theme, for the sermon concludes with an exhortation to loyalty in which David and Christ are the overt subjects and the present-day Davidic king the implicit third term.[65]

Covenantal history is combined with the typology of kingship in Pierce's sermon as it is in Boteler's. The evidence of Restoration satires in general and *Absalom and Achitophel* in particular underscores the Puritan identification with covenantal history. Pierce's sermon betrays the uneasy conjunction of England and Israel in its consciousness that the English are Israelites not only in their election but also in their backsliding and murmuring. Yet the basic assumption on which the structure of identifications rests—that the English are Israelites—was shared by the elegists of Elizabeth I, the panegyrists of Charles II, and the Restoration satirists. However, the circumstances of history and the insistence of politics forced the meaning of this identification to become more complex. The evidence of *Absalom and Achitophel* justifies this contention.[66]

Themes of renewal in nature and art, together with imagery of classical heroism and biblical sanctity, are invoked with predictable, indeed mechanical, regularity in the literature that forms the immediate context for Dryden's *Astraea Redux* and *To His Sacred Majesty*. In Rachel Jevon's *Exultationis Carmen* the figures of Astraea, Tellus, and Phoebus are summoned for the golden age, "Since you, our Faiths Defender, are return'd." [67] But intermixed with classical deities are biblical figures and events that regularly inform political and historical affairs. England is Israel or Canaan; God's work in the Restoration is paralleled with biblical events like the passage through the Red Sea or the destruction of Jericho; and Charles himself figures prominently as David. Francis Gregory, for example, preached a sermon of thanksgiving for Charles II entitled *David's returne from his banishment*.[68] And Dryden, of course, included the Davidic parallel in *Astraea Redux* (ll. 79–82). The recourse to this parallel, however, was not simply based on a fortuitous resemblance between the careers of the two kings; rather, it relied on the long tradition of typological analogy for its justification and, in part, for its meaning.

Henry King's coronation sermon underscores the currency of biblical typology at the Restoration. Applying his text from Ezekiel 21:27 to the present day, King writes:

> Yet this particular of my Text is Mystically interpreted of *Christ,* by whose Copy Kings hold their Right, *All dominion being given to Him,* and from him derived upon *His* Vice-Gerents here in Earth.
> And it may Prophetically and properly enough look on *Zerubbabel* that excellent Prince, who was a *Type of Christ* too; whom, after a long interruption of the Regal Line, God raised up to *rebuild the walls of Hierusalem,* and *Repair the breaches of his Temple.* To which end he threatneth an *Overthrow to the strength of Kingdoms* which should oppose his work of Restauration.

I shall take the liberty, and that without violence to the words, or distorsion of the sense, to apply them unto the happy occasion of *This Day,* and to reflect from hence upon the Calamities suffered under Those who sought to hinder It.[69]

The language of King's sermon is perhaps more circumspect than that of some sermons, but the dynamics of typological analogy are clearly stated and familiar. The king holds his right by virtue of being Christ's copy; the concept of Christomimesis links the present-day monarch with the antitype and with the Old Testament types. Like contemporary divines and like the earlier Stuart elegists, King was familiar with the language of typology and felt at perfect ease in bringing the concept of typological kingship to bear on the present-day monarch.

Combining the typology of kingship and the paralleling of biblical and English history, Elkanah Settle used the language of copy and mold to invoke the divinity of Charles II's kingship: "As God to Monarchs his own Mould does bring, / And in his own bright Image stamps the King; / Sure when to *Charles* th' Almighty Impression came, / . . . So much the Figure of the Son he wrot, / The Fathers Godhead was almost forgot." [70] Like other panegyrists, Settle wished to reunite the generalities of Israelite history with the specific identity of the king as type of Christ. The typology of kingship and covenantial history made an uneasy peace in the literature of the Restoration, as, indeed, the Stuart monarchy made an uneasy peace with Parliamentarian government.

From the Restoration to the end of the seventeenth century occasional poetry continued to make significant use of Old Testament figures and events as analogues and correlative types. They are used copiously both in the elegies occasioned by the death of Charles II and, a few years later, in the poems welcoming William and Mary.[71] Nor had the language of scriptural narrative entirely run its course by the end of the century. In the occasional verse on Queen Anne, Old Testament figure and event are amply used; and in a poem on George I's accession in 1714, Richard Chapman still felt the propriety of greeting the king as "*Moses* ent'ring, with his budding Wand, / Our Laws to settle, and our Hosts command." [72]

But the pulse of scriptural allusion weakened in eighteenth-century England. At about 1700 there was a general shift from typological to analogical interpretation, and by the middle of the eighteenth century traditional typology had greatly changed, the assumptions on which it was based undermined by rational criticism of the Bible.[73] Indeed, Peter Annet was prompted to write his *History of the Man After God's Own Heart* (1761), a biography of King David and a vindication of George II, by panegyrics comparing the late monarch's life to David's. "Comparisons are frequently said to be odious," Annet declared, "but no one was ever more so." [74] An imagination like Blake's would be needed before the terms of biblical history and scriptural typology could be reworked into a new myth for England.

3 THE KING AND CHRIST

Dryden's Restoration panegyrics—*Astraea Redux* and *To His Sacred Majesty*—cannot boast an altogether high critical reputation. The style of the poems, especially Dryden's language of compliment, has puzzled and disturbed readers of more than one generation. In the eighteenth century Samuel Johnson censured the "meanness and servility" of Dryden's "hyperbolical adulation"; and nineteenth-century editors like Sir Walter Scott and Richard Hooper remarked on Dryden's confusion of metaphor and quaintness of expression. Nor have twentieth-century readers expressed more certain delight. Mark Van Doren finds *Astraea Redux* "shapeless and profuse"; and even James Kinsley, in his measured praise of Dryden's panegyrics, declares that *Astraea Redux* swings "between ludicrous exaggeration and the majestic assertion of high ideals." In the most recent criticism, Earl Miner finds the accommodation of classical and biblical elements in *Astraea Redux* incomplete and the control of historical perspective in *To His Sacred Majesty* uneven.[1]

The modest reputation of these poems is explained in part by their genre, the political panegyric having no modern analogue; but it is also due to a neglect by critics of the language spoken by Dryden and his contemporaries when praising kings. It is well known that such devotional poets of the earlier seventeenth century as Donne and Herbert were familiar with the fundamentals and many of the subtleties of figuralism, and that Milton used his ample knowledge of typology to structure his interpretation of Christian history in *Paradise Lost* and *Paradise Regained*.[2] However, the political poets of the interregnum and Restoration periods were also very much aware of typological interpretations of the Old Testament and skilled in the application of typology to contemporary events. To ignore this is to diminish one's appreciation of later seventeenth-century verse and one's understanding of a main current of seventeenth-century thought.[3]

A well-developed tradition of political typology extends from the work of elegists and encomiasts of Elizabeth and James I through the political poetry of King, Cleveland, Marvell, and Dryden. Not only did poets writing in this tradition make use of the familiar reading of Old Testament figures and events as prefigurings of christic phenomena—a practice found in the poetry of Donne and Herbert—they also insisted that contemporary public figures and events shadowed christic phenomena. Thus the civil war could be presented as a correlative of the Flood, each event pointing typologically to the redemptive and cleansing powers of baptism; and the English monarch could be celebrated as a correlative of an Old Testament king, each being a type of Christ in his regal office.

Dryden's commendatory piece *To my Honored Friend, Sir Robert Howard, On his Excellent Poems* sheds some light on the typological aspects of his Restoration panegyrics. It has been observed that the poem to Howard belongs to a "variety of poetry that was never tied to the requirements of sober truth"; and even Howard's recent and admiring biographer seems slightly embarrassed by Dryden's effusiveness.[4] Yet the poem tells a good deal about Dryden's panegyrical language, his attitude toward Charles II, and his knowledge of the Christian accommodation of classical myth:

> Your curious Notes so search into that Age,
> When all was fable but the sacred Page,
> That since in that dark night we needs must stray,
> We are at least misled in pleasant way.
> But what we most admire, your Verse no lesse
> The Prophet than the Poet doth confesse.
> Ere our weak eyes discern'd the doubtfull streak
> Of light, you saw great *Charls* his morning break.
> So skilfull Sea-men ken the Land from far,
> Which shews like mists to the dul Passenger.

To *Charls* your Muse first pays her dutious love,
As still the Antients did begin from *Jove*.

[83–94]

Notable is the careful distinction between fable and sacred history that Dryden makes (l. 84), as well as his reference to the "curious Notes" that Howard prepared for his translation of Statius's *Achilleid*. In part, these notes were intended to accommodate pagan myth to sacred history by showing connections between stories from classical mythology and their biblical counterparts. For example, Howard accepts the identification of Saturn with Noah and points out the similarity of religious ceremonials mentioned in Juvenal and Suetonius to those referred to in the Old Testament.[5] This accommodation of pagan myth to sacred history was, of course, common in mid-seventeenth-century England; the tradition is exemplified in Milton's *On the Morning of Christ's Nativity*.[6] The reference to Howard's "curious Notes," however, removes any doubt that Dryden was familiar with the tradition. Indeed, more than one of his early literary acquaintances was busy combining the biblical and the classical. Dryden's tribute to John Hoddesdon, *To his friend the Authour, on his divine Epigrams,* praises exactly this merging of the biblical and the classical in Hoddesdon's book, *Sion and Parnassus*.

Finally, Dryden praises Howard's *Panegyrick to the king* as revealing the prophet no less than the poet (l. 88), praise that is coupled with an analogy between Charles II and Jove (ll. 93–94). The reference to Howard as a prophet can be explained on the ground that Howard's panegyric was supposedly written three years before the Restoration. But an additional sense of *prophet* is invoked by the analogy between Charles and Jove; for, in the classical and biblical sense, the prophet not only foresaw events but, more importantly, was the spokesman of a deity. The prophet communicated with the god and in turn became the source of knowledge that carried the god's admonitions and promises. In biblical prophecy God's promises often deal with the condition or fate of the community. Thus, for example, Nathan assures David of the continuity of his kingship and reiterates God's pledge of national stability in 2 Samuel. Similarly, Virgil's prophetic vision in the *Aeneid* of the Augustan order (6. 791 ff.) carries the promise of national stability with overtones of harmony and fertility. Dryden's analogy between Charles and Jove suggests that poets and prophets of the present day will draw their inspiration from Charles and create visions of national harmony and fertility in his name, as they once did in Jove's or Jehovah's. In the poem to Howard the divine analogy is drawn cautiously in a simile. But when Dryden later takes up that "Mantle" and "right to prophesy" (ll. 101–2) to celebrate Charles and the Stuart monarchy, he will transform the tentative approach of the simile into the firm conviction of metaphor and type.

Astraea Redux

The Virgilian echoes in *Astraea Redux* (1660)—particularly the messianic imagery drawn from the *Pollio* and from the sixth book of the *Aeneid,* with which the king is greeted—clearly confirm the prophetic role in which Dryden had earlier cast Howard and in which, by the time of *Astraea Redux,* he saw himself as well. Dryden's consciousness of the role of poet as prophet surely informed his understanding of his role as mythographer of the Stuart monarchy. As a spokesman for a divine order and harmony, he was sensitive to the recurring pattern of anticipation and fulfillment, familiar with the vocabulary of typology, and responsive to the providential manner in which current history repeats the past.

Unlike *Absalom and Achitophel,* with its obvious biblical metaphor, or *To His Sacred Majesty,* with its concise scriptural opening, *Astraea Redux* moves obliquely to include English politics in the paradigm of sacred history. The king's exile and return are set in a context that allows for a gradual interpretation of these events as a reflection of biblical history and of Christ's life and resurrection. Dryden begins to establish this pattern with an analogy appropriate to both the classical and Christian motifs of the poem. He then moves through a series of allusions to Christ and specific biblical analogies toward a clearly marked divine analogy that leaves no doubt as to his intent in invoking the christic model for Charles's return to England in 1660.

The pattern of exile and return begins with a reference to Typhon and Jove—a pagan myth, yet one with an important Christian meaning for Dryden's seventeenth-century audience:

> Thus when the bold *Typhoeus* scal'd the Sky,
> And forc'd great *Jove* from his own Heaven to fly,
> (What King, what Crown from Treasons reach is free,
> If *Jove* and *Heaven* can violated be?)
>
> [37–40]

The comparison is between Typhon striking at Jove and the English mob rebelling against the king. The choice of Typhon's rebellion as a representation of the English rebellion is of particular interest, for Typhon had not only been allegorized in general political terms,[7] but he had also been chosen to provide a classical counterpart to Satan's rebellion against God. Milton, for example, refers to Typhon in *Paradise Lost* (1. 192–200), making specific the connection between the pagan giant and the Christian devil. Indeed, Renaissance mythographers had made the rebellious Titans a commonplace *topos* for allegorical treatment, so that by midseventeenth century the myth of Typhon's rebellion against the deities clearly suggested Satan's rebellion against God.[8] Dryden also bends this myth toward his own day by emphasizing the motif of exile (ll. 41–42). Between Satan and God and the English and Charles, Dryden places the classical myth that can give in both directions.

Dryden then turns specifically to the king (l. 49), and for ninety lines his chief concern is to portray the monarch in exile. Although Charles is not portrayed exclusively as a christic figure, there is persuasive evidence that he is being identified with Christ:

> How Great were then Our *Charles* his Woes, who thus
> Was forc'd to suffer for Himself and us!
>
> .   .   .   .
>
> Heir to his Fathers Sorrows, with his Crown,
> Could tast no sweets of youths desired Age,
> But found his life too true a Pilgrimage.
>
> [49–54]

Dryden's next allusion is to Enoch and Elijah, which, read in a typological context, clearly reinforces the implied identification of Charles with Christ:

> As Souls reach Heav'n while yet in Bodies pent,
> So did he live above his Banishment.
>
> [59–60]

Enoch and Elijah, who were translated to heaven as a reward for their sinless lives, are the "Souls." As a simple analogy, Enoch and Elijah's earthly lives among the ungodly are being compared to Charles's life in exile. As Enoch and Elijah rose above the limitations of their carnal natures, so Charles rose above the limitation of his banishment with the virtues of character that distinguished his biblical analogues: patience, courage, and wisdom.[9]

That is one explanation of the analogy, but a relationship between biblical and contemporary figures is often not based simply on analogous personal characteristics. For seventeenth-century biblical commentators Enoch and Elijah were types of Christ and the Resurrection. For the commentator John Richardson, Elijah was a "pledge and pawne of the Resurrection, and life eternal and celestial, and prophesied of the last and general judgment."[10] Furthermore, as the biblical characters figurally represent Christ's resurrection, so Charles's restoration is a reflection thereof. The inclusion of Charles in this paradigm is strengthened by Dryden's repeated allusions and references to Charles's christic nature (ll. 52–54; 71–72; 139–40; 240–41; 288–89). The typological significance of Enoch and Elijah activates the model of Christ's resurrection with reference to the Restoration. As the nation is the

Virgin Bride of Charles (ll. 19–20), as the king renews nature (ll. 129–36, 292–95), so too his restoration is a recapitulation of the Resurrection. Astraea, David, Charles, and Christ all suffer banishment and return in greater glory. The act is repeated time and again in history, and the individual event— Charles's restoration, in this case—takes meaning both from its position in a recurring scheme and from the greater paradigm it shadows.

However, while the relationship between Enoch and Elijah and Charles II has a christological center, that center is not the focus of the analogy. The focus is, of course, Charles. In political poetry, typological analogy invokes the greater paradigm in order to inform the event at hand. The significance of the Resurrection, with its associations of renewal and glorious rebirth, is quite consciously manipulated by Dryden in *Astraea Redux*. It is not simply hyperbolic flattery to see the Restoration in the terms Dryden chooses; rather, it is an exercise of historical consciousness, an attempt to understand the present in terms of the past, particularly in terms of the sacred past with its special meanings.

In the couplet following the allusion to Enoch and Elijah, Dryden seems to change the metaphor by comparing Charles to a sun that interregnum England saw only in reflected glory: "That Sun which we beheld with cous'ned eyes / Within the water, mov'd along the skies" (ll. 61–62). Unrelated on a literal level there is nonetheless a connection between the couplets; for, while the second couplet does not extend the terms of correlative typology, it does depend on typology as a frame of reference. According to seventeenth-century typologists, the coming of Christ had been promised through shadowy types and figures that suggested, but did not reveal, the full glory of the antitype. The apprehension of Christ in the Old Testament and then under the New Dispensation moves, as Milton phrases it, "from shadowy Types to Truth." [11] So, too, Charles was seen only with "cous'ned eyes" during the interregnum; his full glory is visible only after the Restoration. The link between Charles and Christ is strengthened through the metaphor of the sun, a common symbol of Christ in the

New Testament and in biblical commentary. Moreover, the metaphor identifies the English with the Israelites, a comparison that Dryden often makes in his later poetry. If during Charles's banishment the English beheld the type of Christ only in reflection, then they were participating in sacred history, repeating the story of the Israelites who beheld Christ in shadowy forms. The identification of the English with the Israelites is made obliquely; but, with knowledge of the ways in which Dryden later develops this identification, its genesis can be seen.

As Dryden proceeds with his portrait of the king in exile, he reiterates the connection between Charles and Christ and draws further biblical analogies. After both regretting and blessing the king's sufferings (1. 72), Dryden makes what is to become a familiar comparison between Charles and David (1. 79). The comparison of the figures is relatively light in tone, yet in selecting details for the analogy Dryden carefully emphasizes David's divine anointment. As with Dryden's later use of that motif, the association of David with Charles is an occasion both for witty paralleling and for invoking the more serious, sanctifying power implied by David's divine kingship.

Then the identification of the king with Christ is explicitly made:

> The Prince of Peace would like himself confer
> A gift unhop'd without the price of war.

> [139–40]

And Charles, Christlike, calms the waters on the voyage home:

> The same indulgence *Charles* his Voyage bless'd
> Which in his right had Miracles confess'd.

> [240–41]

Finally, toward the end of *Astraea Redux*, Dryden mentions Charles's nativity in a context that leaves no doubt that he also alludes to Christ's:

> That Star that at your Birth shone out so bright
> It stain'd the duller Suns Meridian light.

> [288–89]

This is, of course, an "obvious allusion to the Star of Bethle-
hem." [12] "Other poems written on the same occasion" suggest
that Dryden's contemporaries "did not find the flattery inde-
corous, or the comparison of the King with the Saviour shock-
ing and distasteful." [13] Indeed, not only did other poems on
the Restoration conflate the king with Christ, but earlier sermons and poems, elegies and epitaphs on Elizabeth, Prince
Henry, James I, and Charles I had made the comparison of
prince with Savior an important traditional element in panegyrical literature.

In the closing section of the poem the emphasis on Charles's
divine kingship turns from the monarch as suffering servant
to a presentation of him in terms of both christic mercy and
Jehovic authority. The transformation begins with the cliffs
of Albion reaching out to greet the king:

> As you meet it, the Land approacheth you.
> The Land returns, and in the white it wears
> The marks of penitence and sorrow bears.
>
> [253–55]

The language of sin and expiation in these lines recalls
Christ's sacrifice, as does the next couplet: "But you, whose
goodness your discent doth show, / Your Heav'nly Parentage
and earthly too." Dryden is playing on the several meanings
of "discent" to suggest the sacrifice of banishment, the greater
sacrifice of Christ's descent into the flesh, Charles II's descent
from Charles I, and, as heaven's anointed king, his descent
from God. Yet, having recalled Charles in exile, Dryden next
begins to transform him from a correlative type, who, along
with Enoch and Elijah, activates the paradigm of Christ's
sacrifice, into a figure that embodies the power and authority
of God the Father:

> Not ty'd to rules of Policy, you find
> Revenge less sweet then a forgiving mind.
> Thus when th'Almighty would to *Moses* give
> A sight of all he could behold and live;
> A voice before his entry did proclaim
> *Long-Suff'ring, Goodness, Mercy* in his Name.

> Your Pow'r to Justice doth submit your Cause,
> Your Goodness only is above the Laws;
> Whose rigid letter while pronounc'd by you
> Is softer made.
>
> [260–69]

In the first couplet Dryden asserts the merciful quality of Charles's mind; then, in the next two couplets, he specifically likens Charles's merciful treatment of the English (the Act of Oblivion, which Charles was known to favor before his restoration) to God's treatment of Moses and, by extension, of the Israelites. The last three lines extend the analogy between Charles and God, suggesting that as God renews his covenant with the Israelites through the Law, so, too, Charles will renew his covenant with the English, forgiving past iniquities and tempering power with justice and goodness. The historical reference again is to the Act of Oblivion, but Dryden is dealing with more than history. In pronouncing the letter of the law, Charles reflects the authority of God the Father; yet, as a type of Christ, he also transforms the law, completing the covenant of the written word with the covenant of mercy. The phrase "rigid letter" is an allusion to the Mosaic covenant, the tablets of stone; "softer" pronunciation surely alludes to the covenant of mercy, written in the tablets of the heart. Thus, in his restoration, Charles exemplifies the twin aspects of divine kingship: authority and mercy. The king as Christ the healer and savior, the suffering servant, is prominent in the first part of the poem; but with the actual return (ll. 250 ff.) the presentation of the king broadens, so that, as restored ruler, he may represent both merciful healer and lawgiver.[14]

The poem closes with the renewal of nature, a reference to Charles's nativity star, and a Virgilian welcome to a new golden age. That vision of the future—"times whiter Series is begun" (l. 292)—does not simply result from the application of a classical myth to a contemporary event but evolves from several sources: the interaction of classical and Christian myth; the typological identification of Charles with Christ;

the transformation of that figure into an image combining Old Testament authority and New Testament mercy—in sum, from the ability to see contemporary history as an extension and repetition of sacred history.

To His Sacred Majesty

In *To His Sacred Majesty,* published in 1661, a year after *Astraea Redux,* Dryden again finds use for biblical narrative, classical allusion, and a considerable amount of historical detail; but the texture and strategy of *To His Sacred Majesty* differ. Rather than interweaving biblical and classical imagery with historical event, Dryden separates them: the opening is biblical narrative; the coronation proper has biblical overtones but is pictorial in method; and the presentation of the king is heavily historical with only an occasional reference to classical figures. Yet the biblical imagery is central to Dryden's purpose. The typological perspective of the poem's opening scenes creates an important setting for the presentation of the king's coronation as a sacred event.

Dryden begins in the past tense of scriptural history with the Deluge, the sighting of dry land, and the wait for the renewal of nature (ll. 1–8). Then Charles is addressed in the present tense—"Thus (Royall Sir) to see you landed here" (l. 9). The first set of associations is complete: the Deluge is the civil war; the drowned world is England; the antediluvian sinners are Commonwealth Englishmen; the ark is the ship that returned the king to England; and Noah is Charles II. The correspondences are clear, but what is to be made of their relationship? How is one to understand Charles as Noah or the English as those wicked generations of Adam drowned in the Flood?

It has been argued that Dryden is working in analogies—that the Flood is a "conventional description of rebellion" and that the identification of Charles with Noah provides a starting point for Dryden's patriarchalist theory in defense of monarchy.[15] But that does not explain why the passage from Genesis has overtones particularly appropriate to Dryden's presentation of the return and coronation of the king. For Dryden conceives of the king as an instrument of God in the preservation of a chosen people, and this conception is only possible when the analogy is read in terms of sacred history. The figural relationship that Noah bears to Christ sharpens Charles's salvific image; it prepares the reader for Charles's role as gift of manna and divinely anointed Davidic king, and for his ability to renew nature and restore the church. The figural relationship between Noah and Charles through Christ also enhances the idea of the English as a sinful yet covenanted people. Charles and Noah, as correlative types, reflect Christ's power to renew time and repair the ruins of sin; Charles repeats scriptural history and foreshadows events of the Christian millennium. Noah's role as savior of the elect is echoed in Charles's renewal of the church. And perhaps the patriarch's task of fathering a new race is involved at the close of the poem, as the speaker asks Charles to insure the happiness and security of the nation through marriage and offspring.

As for the specific typological significance of the opening passage, the Deluge of the first line is not only a historical event—not only a conventional image of rebellion—but also a judgment on the people. As William Guild wrote: "In the daies of *Noah,* defection from true Religion, oppression, sensuality, and security, after 1656 years, brought on the first destruction on the world. *So the like sins now reigning, about the like time, is like to bring on the second Judgement on the latter world.*" [16] Though Dryden was writing from a different political perspective, by identifying the civil war with the Flood he established the same providential reading of contemporary events. The civil war was a judgment on the people, but through Noah-Charles the covenant will be restored. Noah's role in the story of the Flood, especially when seen in its typological perspective, has important associations for the role that Charles II plays in *To His Sacred Majesty.* Through Noah, man's ancient dominion over the creatures is partially restored; he is an instrument of God in repairing the ruins of the antediluvian world. Thomas Taylor, in *Moses and Aaron,* effectively summarized the typology of Noah and Christ, showing how both repair the world, replenish earth and heaven, preserve and provide for all creatures, and exact a mild obedience from savage forces.[17]

Taylor's commentary and others like it suggest not that Dryden was using every figural potential of the biblical patriarch but, rather, that Noah, through an exegetical tradition still alive in seventeenth-century England, had figural characteristics that could be drawn on to suit the needs of the poet. Charles, as Noah's correlative, shared those characteristics. The figural aspect does not shift the focus of the poem to Christ but does enhance the significance of English history. Thus Charles can be seen in terms of Christ's sacrifice for a sinful people, and he can suggest the character of authority and lawful justice epitomized by the God of Abraham and Isaac.

As numerous figural characteristics had become associated with Noah, so, too, the ark was one of the most frequently explicated Old Testament types. The ark in troubled waters was a figure of the church; and as an instrument of salvation it often typified Christ. Much of Augustine's intense, detailed explication of the ark as Christ was adopted by seventeenth-century English typology manuals.[18] But in *To His Sacred Majesty* detail is less important than the general figural significance. Noah, the ark, and the Flood all had familiar and important Christian meanings for the seventeenth-century reader. As instruments of divine judgment and salvation they were logical choices for Dryden's rendering of the English salvation.

From scriptural history, Dryden turns to the present day and extends his portrait of the king in ostensibly ordinary images:

Thus (Royall Sir) to see you landed here
Was cause enough of triumph for a year:
Nor would your care those glorious Joyes repeat

Till they at once might be secure and great:
Till your kind beams by their continu'd stay
Had warm'd the ground, and call'd the Damps away.
Such vapours while your pow'rfull influence dryes
Then soonest vanish when they highest rise.

[9–16]

The likening of the king to the sun was traditional in poems
on James I and Charles I.[19] Yet there is a connection between
the biblical imagery and the familiar sun metaphor. In *To
His Sacred Majesty,* as in *Astraea Redux,* the metaphor has
distinctly christic overtones. Benjamin Keach's Τροπολογια: *A
Key To Open Scripture Metaphors* (1682) systematizes a group
of common seventeenth-century associations, among them the
sun as an appropriate metaphor for Christ, who, "appearing
and rising upon the Soul, drives away and expells Darkness,
turns Night into Day, and scatters all the Clouds and black
Mists of Sin, Ignorance, and Unbelief, in the Soul." [20] As Keach
"opens" the metaphor, the language becomes strikingly similar to that of *To His Sacred Majesty.* The parallels include
damps, vapors, guilty months, and tainted years. The language of sin and expiation in *To His Sacred Majesty* suggests
that Charles metaphorically has many of the same powers that
Keach attributes to Christ. The christic overtones do not
complicate the metaphor but, rather, clarify the relationships
of Charles as Noah, Charles as the sun, and Charles as the
source of renewal in nature and religion.

The first verse paragraph of *To His Sacred Majesty* closes
with a couplet that completes the explicitly biblical section of
the poem:

We had not yet exhausted all our store
When you refresh'd our joyes by adding more:
As Heav'n of old dispenc'd Caelestial dew,
You give us Manna and still give us new.

[21–24]

The Restoration and the coronation provide two sources of
joy; and as the Restoration was expressed through biblical

metaphor, so the coronation is manna to the children of England. Like the episode from Genesis, the story of the Israelites in the desert was the focus of much commentary and exegesis. God's gift of manna was read as a sign of beneficence toward his special people—of patience and love, watchfulness and care "to his Church, both Jewish and Christian, and to all the Israel of God, Legal and Evangelical"; more specifically, manna was read as a type of Christ. The story's figural meaning has been summarized by Thomas Taylor:

> When Israel had great need of Gods help, and had no power to help themselves, when they were even ready to starve: Even so when the Church was in extream need of Christ, and altogether helplesse in her self, it pleased God to give his Sonne from heaven to save and refresh her. . . . Then God gave Israel Manna, when Israel (murmuring) had deserved nothing but wrath and vengeance.[21]

Read back into Dryden's text, the typological aspect of the Old Testament narrative enhances the significance of the metaphor. The coronation as gift of manna is not simply biblical analogy but analogy informed by typological meaning, which locates the contemporary event in the pattern of providential history, suggesting its eternality. As Charles's coronation repeats God's gift of manna, so the English in their forwardness, deserving the rod and fire, repeat the history of the Israelites wandering in the desert. Although these two scriptural motifs—Israel's forwardness and God's refreshing mercy—are suggested here and echoed in such phrases as "our sad ruines" (l. 25), the full development of both halves of the narrative must wait for *Absalom and Achitophel;* for the emphasis in *To His Sacred Majesty* is on Charles as an affirmation of God's gift to the Israelites—his watchfulness over the chosen people.

First presented as Noah and the gift of manna, Charles, in the second verse paragraph, becomes "not King of us alone but of the year," transformed from a principle of salvation into an instrument of renewal:

Now our sad ruines are remov'd from sight,
The Season too comes fraught with new delight;
Time seems not now beneath his years to stoop
Nor do his wings with sickly feathers droop.

[25–28]

The "sad ruines" are at once England of 1661 and the post-diluvian remains of the ancient world. The theme of renewal in nature unites the earlier motifs of regeneration after the Flood with the spring of 1661 and the harmony in church and state that Charles's coronation promises. The opening of the second verse paragraph looks back to the earlier biblical scene and forward to Dryden's rendering of the coronation:

Next to the sacred Temple you are led,
Where waites a Crown for your more sacred Head:
How justly from the Church that Crown is due,
Preserv'd from ruine and restor'd by you!

[45–48]

Charles as preserver and renewer of the church surely has christic overtones. His divine energy is felt in the natural and spiritual worlds and by the end of the poem promises England's future happiness. Biblical and natural metaphors reinforce one another and have divine, and at times christic, overtones.

The consideration of the coronation proper (ll. 49 ff.) turns from the metaphor of biblical history to the detail of visual and aural spectacle. Yet the scene permits allusion to Davidic kingship and creates a specific analogy between Charles as sovereign and God as monarch of heaven. While the king is installed with a ceremony reminiscent of those in the Old Testament, the people "employ / Our time like Angels in expressing joy" (ll. 67–68). Like God, the king is sufficient unto himself: "Not that our wishes do increase your store, / Full of your self you can admit no more" (ll. 65–66). The analogy between royal attendants and angels, as well as the assertion of the king's perfect essence, clearly suggests the divinity of Charles's kingship. The language of perfection and completeness echoes the traditional Christian understanding of the perfect wholeness of God.[22]

The biblical elements in the remainder of the portrait are modified in the direction of secular expression; yet even an allusion to the king's improvements in St. James Park (ll. 111 ff.) is enhanced by the poem's opening lines. The king's dominion over fish and fowl—his protection of natural life— is colored by the figure of Noah, with whom Charles is first identified. But the explicitly biblical is not woven through the text with repeated allusion. The two biblical references at the opening and close of the first verse paragraph establish a frame of reference for reading the entire poem. The movement from preservation to regeneration, which is accomplished by imagery from nature and by fragments of Old Testament narrative, reflects a story of divine intervention. The typical aspect of God's saving his chosen people is repeated throughout time. Biblical narrative read typologically gives a cosmic importance to the characters and events of English history. Indeed, unless the connection is made between the sacred history of the past and the sacred history of the present, the analogies in *To His Sacred Majesty* are only hyperbole and exaggeration.

4 REDEMPTIVE HISTORY

The Restoration panegyrics were Dryden's first attempt to set English political life in a scriptural context,[1] but between the writing of the panegyrics and the creation of *Absalom and Achitophel* he often returned to the scriptural perspective. In *To My Lord Chancellor* (1662) Dryden presents the king as divine monarch, echoing the Davidic motif of the panegyrics and the solar imagery of *To His Sacred Majesty*. The more secular references to temples and to kings as earthly gods in *To my Honour'd Friend, Dr. Charleton* (1663) support the tenets of government found in Dryden's Restoration panegyrics and in his political poems of the 1680s.[2] However, Dryden's most ambitious poem of this period, and the one that most fully invokes the scriptural perspective, is *Annus Mirabilis*.

Annus Mirabilis

Dryden's use of scriptural allusions and references in *Annus Mirabilis* (1667) to create a salvific identity for the king and a redemptive history for the nation clearly links the poem both to his earlier and to his later political poetry. The scriptural perspective not only gives the events of "The Year of Wonders, 1666" a providential cast that enhances king and court;[3] it also permits Dryden to identify the fortunes of the English with those of the Israelites in combat, judgment, and redemption, and to associate the king with David and Christ—a primary strategy in Dryden's earlier presentation of Charles II and of central importance to the dialectic of *Absalom and Achitophel*.

The title itself foreshadows the apocalyptic motif of the poem's close, but twice in the dedicatory "Verses to her Highness the Dutchess" Dryden refers to Exodus for scriptural analogy. The setting of the naval battle that the verses commemorate is likened to the Red Sea, divided at Israel's exodus (Exod. 14:21–22); and Albemarle sustained by the duchess is compared to Moses sustained by Aaron and Hur, leading the Israelites in victorious battle against the Amalekites (Exod. 17:11–13). In the dedicatory verses, as in the poem proper, Dryden is creating a redemptive history: the Dutch are the Egyptians and the Amalekites; the English are the Jews delivered from the hands of a powerful enemy, God having assured them of salvation through a leader "chosen and appointed by him for an instrument of his grace." [4]

The providential interpretation of historical events in *Annus Mirabilis* begins with the British ships gathering for battle:

> To see this Fleet upon the Ocean move
>   Angels drew wide the Curtains of the skies:
> And Heav'n, as if there wanted Lights above,
>   For Tapers made two glareing Comets rise.
>
> [61–64]

Then, after theorizing about the origin of these two comets, Dryden wonders if one of them is

>   that bright companion of the Sun,
> Whose glorious aspect seal'd our new-born King;
> And now a round of greater years begun,
>   New influence from his walks of light did bring.
>
> [69–72]

As in *Astraea Redux* (ll. 288–91), the mention of the nativity sign is clearly an allusion to Christ, both royal nativities having been marked by a star of special brightness. The association of the king with Christ activates, through the reference to renewed time (l. 71), the motif of redemptive history and anticipates the fuller development of Charles's salvific meaning in the "King's Prayer" (sts. 262–87).

In the descriptions of sea battles that follow Dryden twice invokes scriptural analogy. First, Albemarle's cannon fire is compared to the pillar and the cloud—a return to the earlier identification of Albemarle with Moses:

> His fiery Canon did their passage guide,
>   And foll'wing smoke obscur'd them from the foe.
> Thus *Israel* safe from the *Egyptian*'s pride,
>   By flaming pillars, and by clouds did go.
>
> [365–68]

Then the sinking of a Dutch ship is likened to God's destruction of Uzzah (1 Chron. 13:9–10; 2 Sam. 6:6–7):

> The foe approach'd: and one, for his bold sin,
>   Was sunk, (as he that touch'd the Ark was slain;)
> The wild waves master'd him, and suck'd him in,
>   And smiling Eddies dimpled on the Main.
>
> [373–76]

Both analogies take as their scriptural terms important symbols of God's presence among the Israelites. The pillar and cloud, protecting and guiding the Israelites, and the ark, God's meeting place with man, were commonly read as prefigurations of Christ in his guiding, mediatory, and salvific roles. Moreover, the narratives from which these scriptural types are drawn, combined as they are in *Annus Mirabilis,* telescope history from the desert march to the defeat of the Philistines. The pattern into which Dryden sets the English conflict with the Dutch is the record of God's redemptive power. As Milton had sought to structure history by displaying, at the close of *Paradise Lost* (11. 429–901; 12. 1–605), the recurrent manifestations of divine and satanic forces in Adam's vision and Michael's narration, so Dryden, by invoking the design of providential history, wished to persuade his audience that England's war with the Dutch exemplified the eternal battle between God and Satan. Thus the Dutch, already identified with Israel's enemies, become "like fall'n Angels" who fear the "new *Messiah*'s coming" (ll. 453–54) and like "Fiends" avowing "Miracles" (l. 545), suggesting the devils exorcized by Christ in Luke 4:41.

As Israelites, the English overwhelm their enemies; yet like the Old Testament elect, they are not redeemed by military prowess. The burning of the fleet, the Great Fire, and the scourge of "some dire Usurper Heav'n provides" (l. 849) are afflictions visited on the nation as punishment for past political, and thus moral, deviance. Guided first by a Moses who sustained them in battle, ultimately the English must be redeemed by a divinely anointed king. As David prefigured Christ in his salvific office, so Charles, shadowing Christ, can in that role turn God's wrath away from the people through self-sacrifice. The presentation of Charles in the "King's Prayer" is at once reminiscent of David the psalmist and the christic king of *Astraea Redux,* who, as suffering servant and anointed monarch, assured the redemption of the nation and the renewal of time: [5]

> Mean time he sadly suffers in their grief,
>   Out-weeps an Hermite, and out-prays a Saint:
> All the long night he studies their relief,
>   How they may be suppli'd, and he may want.
>
> O God, said he, thou Patron of my days,
>   Guide of my youth in exile and distress!
> Who me unfriended, brought'st by wondrous ways
>   The Kingdom of my Fathers to possess:
>
> Be thou my Judge, with what unwearied care
>   I since have labour'd for my People's good:
> To bind the bruises of a Civil War,
>   And stop the issues of their wasting bloud.
>
>   .   .   .   .
>
> The Father of the people open'd wide
>   His stores, and all the poor with plenty fed:
> Thus God's Annointed God's own place suppli'd,
>   And fill'd the empty with his daily bread.
>   [1041–52; 1141–44]

As the identification of the king with Christ in the Restoration panegyrics culminated in the renewal of time, so the redemptive history of *Annus Mirabilis* fulfills exactly that expectation. God punishes his nation; but, through the intercession of his anointed, God's wrath is turned away, and from destruction comes renewal. Such is the pattern of redemptive history not only in Revelation but also in the Jewish apocalypse.

The vision that closes *Annus Mirabilis* is prefaced by references to astronomical signs of change—a traditional detail from Old Testament prophecy. And the rebuilding of Jerusalem after the Babylonian exile is compared to the reconstruction of London after the Great Fire:

> Not with more constancy the *Jews* of old,
> By *Cyrus* from rewarded Exile sent:
> Their Royal City did in dust behold,
> Or with more vigour to rebuild it went.
>
> [1157–60]

Dryden's vision of a renewed people and a rebuilt London is meant to recall similar visions of renewal in Isaiah and Ezekiel; Jerusalem rebuilt after the Babylonian exile and London restored after the fire are correlative types of that eschatological antitype the Heavenly Jerusalem. Thus in *Annus Mirabilis*—as in Isaiah and Ezekiel but not in Revelation—attention to the restored nation can focus on its flourishing commerce or agriculture—signs of God's special favor for covenanted nations. Indeed, Dryden's prophecy seems to be modeled on the description of Jerusalem's restoration in Isaiah 60. The central themes of Dryden's vision—naval commerce, the foreign enrichment of the nation, and the humbling of former enemies—are the subject of Isaiah 60:5–6 and 8–14. And such details as the gifts of incense and gold brought by London's suitors (l. 1186) and the materials of gold and silver for the new city (l. 1172) are mentioned in analogous contexts in Isaiah 60:6, 9, and 17. The Old Testament apocalypse is appropriate because it not only treats specifically of the renewal of the Israelite nation but also, in Christian commentary, carries the figural promise of the Heavenly Jerusalem. As in *Astraea Redux* and *To His Sacred Majesty*, biblical history does not replace the contemporary subject matter of Dryden's poetry but increases its significance by emphasizing the congruity between the present day, the sacred past, and, at times, the prophetic future.

Absalom and Achitophel

Absalom and Achitophel (1681) is Dryden's fullest and most important exploration of the sacred identities and themes initiated in the Restoration panegyrics and extended in *Annus Mirabilis*.[6] As in the panegyrics, the figural identity of the king is crucial to the meaning of the poem; and, as in *Annus Mirabilis*, the theme of national redemption is of central importance. But in Dryden's political poetry of the 1680s those themes are tempered by a new emphasis on the satanic nature of the enemy coupled with a new recognition of the tensions of political life in Anglo-Judaic Israel. As the satanic enemy and the political tensions become more prominent, the prophetic vision of renewal becomes more remote. *Absalom and Achitophel* demonstrates both Dryden's increased satiric and imaginative energy in exploring the implications of sacred metaphor and his growing awareness that the unregenerate English Israelites might simply refuse to be saved by the Stuart patriarchs.

In *Absalom and Achitophel* the typological meaning of the characters and episodes works in several ways. The primary vehicle is a biblical story, yet much of the force of biblical narrative is directed toward representing political events in Restoration England. These are the two historical poles of the poem, and they bear to each other the relationship of correlative types. But the biblical characters themselves also have typological meanings that enlarge their importance within the biblical frame and that carry over into the contemporary frame. Furthermore, the contemporary story participates in the symbolic mode of the poem because it is a current manifestation of an eternal ordering of events. Thus the poem has two historical poles and a symbolic mode that is realized through both biblical and Restoration history.

In seventeenth-century scriptural commentary, the narrative of David and Absalom is read as a figure of the continuous struggle between Christ and Antichrist, good and evil.[7] In such commentary David is first identified with Christ,[8] and from that typological relationship grows the figural character of the whole narrative: the identification of David's kingdom with the church; the relationship between Absalom and Antichrist; the analogy between David's loyal band and Christ's apostles; and the overthrow of Absalom and prophesying of peace in David's kingdom as a figure of the Apocalypse and coming of the New Jerusalem. Dryden is not, of course, writing an allegory of the struggle between God and the Devil; rather, he is using the figural aspect of the biblical narrative to enlarge the meaning of his subject and is engaging his reader in a gradual assent to this figural significance by demonstrating what the political affairs in the poem mean in terms of the Christian paradigm. In order to fully establish English history in a figural relationship with Old Testament history, Dryden had to develop the sacred identity of the nation itself; and it is at this point that the Puritan insistence on scriptural identity is brought into play.

In a way it was simply Dryden's good luck that the enemies of the king had, a few years before the writing of *Absalom and Achitophel,* insisted that they were English Israelites. More than just an expression of the providential character of history, the identification of England with Israel permitted the development of England as the Promised Land—the political Eden that Dryden so often refers to in his poetry—and at the same time allowed for the association of the English people with the Israelites. For the political satirist, this association often crystallized in those narratives from Old Testament history that showed the Israelites in moods of complaint, rebellion, idolatry, and moral backsliding. The history of God's chosen people as Israelites ends in the hardening of the Mosaic law into a religion of the letter, the displacement of the Mosaic covenant with the advent of Christ, and the Jews' rejection of the New Dispensation through their rejection of Jesus as Messiah. As a nation, the Old Testament Israelites were a type of the Church—God's chosen people under the New Dispensation. In this capacity the Israelites carried the promise of salvation, but under the New Dispensation the Jews (as opposed to the nation of Old Testament Israelites) carried not the promise of salvation but the stigma of nonbelief. Dryden nicely plays on the tension that arises from the opposition of promise and betrayal—the dual nature of Jewish history—by recording for a Christian audience the history of their own time in terms of an Old Testament narrative. The English as Israelites are a correlative type of the Old Testament elect; like the Israelites they are God's pampered people, but they, too, have a propensity for moral and political deviation.

The first portrait of the English-Israelite nation focuses on the details of Jewish political history (ll. 45–84). From a general characterization—"The *Jews,* a Headstrong, Moody, Murmuring race" (l. 45)—Dryden moves back in Old Testament and contemporary time to examples of Jewish political instability: the rejection of Ishbosheth; the restoration of David; and the past designs to melt the king into "that Golden Calf, a State" (l. 66). The phrase "*Adam*-wits" (l. 51) connects the Fall with later rebellions in Jewish history, and Dryden forges the link between political disobedience and satanic temptation in the lines that close the portrait:

> But, when to Sin our byast Nature leans,
> The carefull Devil is still at hand with means;
> And providently Pimps for ill desires:
> The Good old Cause reviv'd, a Plot requires.
> Plots, true or false, are necessary things,
> To raise up Common-wealths, and ruin Kings.
>
> [79–84]

The past tense of Jewish rebellion turns, in these generalizing couplets, to the permanent condition of sin, and typical history becomes archetypal pattern for both the Jewish past and the English present.

The general theme of Jewish political instability is expanded in several places. The murmuring, headstrong race becomes the "giddy *Jews*" who change their Lord by caprice (ll. 216–19). Later their stubbornness is referred to (l. 327), and eventually the regicide that marks both Jewish and English history is recalled:

> Succession, for the general Good design'd,
> In its own wrong a Nation cannot bind:
> If altering that, the People can relieve,
> Better one Suffer, than a Nation grieve.
> The *Jews* well know their power: e'r *Saul* they Chose,
> God was their King, and God they durst Depose.
>
> [413–18]

Achitophel's argument—"Better one Suffer, than a Nation grieve"—is an echo of Caiaphas's argument for the crucifixion of Christ (John 11:50),[9] and the lines that follow move from allusion to direct statement. Although there is an echo of God's comment in 1 Samuel 8:7—"They have rejected me, that I should not reign over them"—there is also an allusion to the deposition of Charles I, whom the English beheaded before they chose Cromwell (Saul).

The murmuring, backsliding element in Jewish history is further detailed through the portraits of the malcontents. Especially in these portraits Dryden emphasizes the identification that the English Puritans claimed with the chosen people of sacred history. A special sect of Israelites is introduced in a brief portrait that is filled with Dryden's peculiar strain of irony and contempt:

> Hot *Levites* Headed these; who pul'd before
> From th'*Ark,* which in the Judges days they bore,
> Resum'd their Cant, and with a Zealous Cry,
> Pursu'd their old belov'd Theocracy.

Where Sanhedrin and Priest inslav'd the Nation,
And justifi'd their Spoils by Inspiration;
For who so fit for Reign as *Aaron's* Race,
If once Dominion they could found in Grace?
These led the Pack; tho not of the surest scent,
Yet deepest mouth'd against the Government.
A numerous Host of dreaming Saints succeed;
Of the true old Enthusiastick breed:
'Gainst Form and Order they their Power employ;
Nothing to Build and all things to Destroy.

[519–32]

In these lines Dryden plays on the contemporary association of Puritan and dissenting ministers with Old Testament zealots. The irony is directed through metaphor and image against the faults of religious hypocrisy and political opportunism. The fruitless zeal of the dissenters, their destructive anger, is caught by such phrases as "Hot *Levites*" and "Zealous Cry," and the description "These led the Pack; tho not of surest scent" reduces the whole "Enthusiastick breed" to roving hounds. The charges of spiritual and political corruption become motifs that Dryden returns to in the individual portraits. Hypocrisy and venality are well-known elements in Shimei's portrait; and the rendering of Corah ironically contrasts the Puritans' self-interest and self-righteous zeal with the true inspiration of the Old Testament prophets.[10]

The details of political instability, regicide, and religious hypocrisy that Dryden combines in his portrait of the Jews culminate in the narrator's apostrophe to the nation: "Oh foolish *Israel!* never warn'd by ill, / Still the same baite, and circumvented still" (ll. 753–54). In the speech that follows Dryden does not so much reiterate the individual crimes of the nation as rely on evidence already established to give the force of concrete detail to his generalizations. The apostrophe repeats, through rhetorical questions and generalized Royalist principles, the argument that is also supplied through the detailed portraits and the dramatic interchange of Absalom and Achitophel. "Foolish *Israel*" is the nation in rebellion.

After presenting Israel's folly at close range and in rhetorical summary, Dryden balances the folly with the hope of renewal through the law and through the king. English as Jewish history culminates with David's transformation from christic mildness to Jehovic authority in the closing speech of the poem.

Absalom and Achitophel begins in the temporally spacious world of Old Testament history. The indeterminate biblical past of the opening lines permits Dryden to set the specific narrative from 2 Samuel in a wide historical frame that suggests the legitimacy of the king's promiscuity by associating the king as father of the land with the patriarchal age, prior to the revelation on Sinai and the institution of priesthood:

> In pious times, e'r Priest-craft did begin,
> Before *Polygamy* was made a sin;
> When man, on many, multiply'd his kind,
> E'r one to one was, cursedly, confind:
> When Nature prompted, and no law deny'd
> Promiscuous use of Concubine and Bride;
> Then, *Israel*'s Monarch, after Heaven's own heart,
> His vigorous warmth did, variously, impart
> To Wives and Slaves: And, wide as his Command,
> Scatter'd his Maker's Image through the Land.
>
> [1–10]

The association between God and David is made through the witty juxtaposition of divine and human fertility. There is, as students of the poem have fully recognized, some irony at work in seeing God's abundant creation reflected in the king's sexual prodigality,[11] but the irony does not reduce the stature of the king. Rather, it serves to separate, at the beginning of the poem, the person of the king from the office of kingship. Some critics of the poem see the transformation of the king from the beginning to the end of the poem as a plea by Dryden that the king abandon his promiscuity and assume the proper godlike authority of a monarch.[12] But the plot of the poem and the various characters argue (with or without their own knowledge) that throughout the poem Charles reflects the godhead; the relationship that exists between the paternal role of the earthly and heavenly monarchs also exists between God as sovereign and the king in his official capacity.

The opening scenes emphasize David as indulgent father, not as head of the country. David's pleasure in Absalom suggests the "beloved son in whom God has been well pleased," [13] but it also recalls God's attitude toward Adam in the Garden. All Absalom's motions are

> accompanied with grace;
> And *Paradise* was open'd in his face.
> With secret Joy, indulgent *David* view'd
> His Youthfull Image in his Son renew'd:
> To all his wishes Nothing he deny'd,
> And made the Charming *Annabel* his Bride.
>
> [29–34]

The natural ease and beauty of Absalom, coupled with the specific reference to Paradise, establish him as the Edenic figure to which Dryden will return in the temptation.[14] In fact, the scene appears to be a reworking of those passages in the eighth book of *Paradise Lost* in which God takes pleasure in seeing and talking to Adam and which culminate in the promise of Eve (8. 449–51). Dryden's characterization of David emphasizes a combination of divine and human paternity. Like God, David takes joy in his creation; like God, he supplies Absalom with a pleasing bride. The serious presentation of David in his paternal joy and indulgence, seen especially against the divine model, can hardly be taken as a condemnation of the monarch. Rather, it strengthens the casual relationship between David and God established at the opening of the poem. When Dryden calls attention to indulgence or weakness in David's character, it is in a context that shows David's indulgence to be a reflection of his paternal, rather than sovereign, capacity:

> What faults he had (for who from faults is free?)
> His Father coud not, or he woud not see.
>
> [35–36]

The emphasis is clearly on David's paternal indulgence. The initial presentation of David and Absalom closes with an assertion of the Edenic calm of David's reign:

> Thus Prais'd, and Lov'd, the Noble Youth remain'd,
> While *David*, undisturb'd, in *Sion* raign'd.
>
> [41–42]

David is again referred to in the introductory lines on the Israelites:

> Those very *Jewes*, who, at their very best,
> Their Humour more than Loyalty exprest,
> Now, wondred why, so long, they had obey'd
> An Idoll Monarch which their hands had made:
> Thought they might ruine him they could create;
> Or melt him to that Golden Calf, a State.
>
> [61–66]

The context in which Dryden sets the epithet "Idoll" is a reflection of the Jews' attitude toward their king. The conception of the king as a product of the people's hands, an idol that can be ruined or created at their will, is contrary to the narrator's attitude (ll. 791–94). For him, David is no "Idoll Monarch" but a skilled and merciful ruler whose kingship exemplifies harmony and balance:

> And *David*'s mildness manag'd it so well,
> The Bad found no occasion to Rebell.
>
> [77–78]

David's prerebellion rule is a reflection of God's rule in Eden before the Fall; at the conclusion of the poem the king's rule typifies God's judicial authority. Rather than being arbitrary and pseudoapocalyptic,[15] the conclusion of the poem is a confirmation of, and a response to, the earlier Edenic state.

The narrator's presentation of David at the opening of the poem is directly and indirectly confirmed when David is seen through the eyes or in the context of his enemies and allies. As Dryden delineates the other characters in the poem, he supports David's typological significance and the figural design of the poem as a whole. In the temptation, Achitophel uses the language of biblical typology to persuade Absalom of his destined kingship. The invocation of Absalom as biblical type and then antitypical completion (l. 240) stands in direct contrast to Achitophel's presentation of David as the fallen Lucifer. Absalom as false Messiah and the political meaning of his false Christhood sharpen the case that Dryden makes for the king as a true reflection of the godhead.

The temptation of Absalom begins with Achitophel's persuasion through biblical types:

> Auspicious Prince! at whose Nativity
> Some Royal Planet rul'd the Southern sky;
> Thy longing Countries Darling and Desire;
> Their cloudy Pillar, and their guardian Fire:
> Their second *Moses,* whose extended Wand
> Divides the Seas, and shews the promis'd Land:
> Whose dawning Day, in every distant age,
> Has exercis'd the Sacred Prophets rage:
> The Peoples Prayer, the glad Deviners Theam,
> The Young-mens Vision, and the Old mens Dream!
> Thee, *Saviour,* Thee, the Nations Vows confess;
> And, never satisfi'd with seeing, bless.
>
> [230–41]

The use of typology in the biblical context of the poem implies a subtle distinction between Absalom's response to the temptation and the reader's response to Achitophel's rhetoric. Absalom cannot know from the evidence of types that he is not the messianic antitype that biblical prophecy heralds; the reader, however, can place the meaning of this temptation in a Christian perspective and judge both the tempter and his victim by the Christian paradigm. By using types to persuade Absalom of his role as savior, Achitophel becomes an ironic Gospel prophet, and Absalom a false messiah. The persuasion begins with the phrase "Auspicious Prince" (l. 230). For Absalom *auspicious* means favored by Fortune, carrying tokens of the divine will. Nor is Achitophel slow to offer specific indications of this augury. He first claims that Absalom's nativity was marked by "some Royal Planet [that] rul'd the Southern sky" (l. 231)—a generally favorable omen.[16] But the astronomical sign, which is one of the messianic allusions of the temptation scene, is not the correct nativity sign for the real Messiah, whose star rises not in the south but in the east (Matt. 2:2, 9–11).

Next Achitophel calls Absalom the country's cloudy pillar, guardian fire, and second Moses (ll. 233–35). All three are familiar typological signs; and the pillar and fire are promised in Isaiah as signs of God's renewed presence among the Israelites (Isa. 4:5). Thus the typological signs that Achitophel invokes have a general biblical integrity and would have been persuasive for Absalom, the biblical prince. Achitophel carefully follows the citation of types with an account of Absalom as the subject of sacred prophecy. The meaning of the typological signs, the prophetic dreams, and the biblical prayers is then quickly realized in Achitophel's apostrophe, "Thee, *Saviour*, Thee, the Nations Vows confess" (l. 240). Having elaborated on Absalom as fulfillment of the messianic types, Achitophel swiftly presses for the political realization of the promise, combining the language and argument of Satan's seduction of Eve in the ninth book of *Paradise Lost* with his temptation of Christ in the third book of *Paradise Regained*.[17] The reader's response to, and judgment of, Achitophel's intentions and allegiances and Absalom's role in the poem are thus informed by the borrowings from Milton, the allusions to Genesis, and the use of typology.

In convincing Absalom of his messianic role, Achitophel portrays David as an old man with declining powers and as a fallen Lucifer:

> Had thus Old *David,* from whose Loyns you spring,
> Not dar'd, when Fortune call'd him, to be King,
> At *Gath* an Exile he might still remain,
> And heavens Anointing Oyle had been in vain.
> Let his successfull Youth your hopes engage,
> But shun th' example of Declining Age:
> Behold him setting in his Western Skies,

The Shadows lengthning as the Vapours rise.
He is not now, as when on *Jordan's* Sand
The Joyfull People throng'd to see him Land,
Cov'ring the *Beach,* and blackning all the *Strand:*
But, like the Prince of Angels from his height,
Comes tumbling downward with diminish'd light.

[262–74]

But a good deal of irony informs this portrait, alerting the reader to Achitophel's deceptive persuasion. Hoping to convince Absalom of the practicability of a "pleasing Rape upon the Crown" (l. 474), Achitophel associates David's old age with his supposed political impotence. Moreover, Achitophel attempts to remove the kingship and the question of succession from the authority of Heaven and the law of God by falsifying the account of David's return from exile. According to Achitophel, David was called from Gath by Fortune; according to Scripture, he was called from exile by God and anointed by Heaven. Achitophel's argument makes the sanctity of Heaven dependent on the arbitrary roll of Fortune's wheel, whose prizes must be seized. In the context of biblical history, that ethic obviously contradicts the moral code and world order implied by God's written law.

The climax of Achitophel's description is the simile "like the Prince of Angels," used to epitomize David's decline. Ostensibly, Achitophel chooses this image to contrast the descending, faltering light of David's kingship with the rising royal planet of Absalom's aspirations; but the use of this simile reveals far more than rhetorical juxtaposition. By identifying godlike David with Satan, Achitophel joins forces with the devil himself (and with Shimei, who is still to appear) as a contemner and blasphemer of God. This reversal of the narrator's view of David is calculated to confirm what the reader knows of Achitophel from the Miltonic overtones of the seduction scene.

As the portrait closes, Achitophel characterizes David's impotence more subtly. Asserting that David is powerless to resist Absalom's claim to the throne, Achitophel asks, "What strength can he to your Designs oppose, / Naked of Friends, and round beset with Foes" (l. 279–80). The second line of the couplet alludes to Samson and suggests Milton's description of Samson blind among enemies:

> Betray'd, Captiv'd, and both my Eyes put out,
> Made of my Enemies the scorn and gaze;
>
> .   .   .   .
>
> Blind among enemies, O worse than chains,
> Dungeon, or beggary, or decrepit age! [18]

There are two ways of reading such an allusion back into Achitophel's portrait of David. The more obvious is that Achitophel unwittingly predicts the final triumph of David as a Samson figure who rains destruction on his enemies and asserts the force of God's law. But, in so describing David, Achitophel is also invoking David's typological relationship to Christ, especially Christ among enemies and false friends. That typological relationship also asserts the final victory of God over Satan and all antichrists. Moreover, David as correlative with Samson, given the typological relationship that both Old Testament figures bear to Christ, plays off nicely against David's own reference to Absalom as a false Samson, a pretended Messiah:

> If my Young *Samson* will pretend a Call
> To shake the Column, let him share the Fall.
>
> [955–56]

The couplet works in two ways, at once characterizing "Absalom's revolt and messianic pretension as a 'fall' " and ironically opposing to it the "true messianic 'call' and 'fall' to sacrifice and death which Samson, as type of Christ, exemplifies." [19] Thus Dryden uses the words of Achitophel and the drama of his temptation of Absalom both to characterize the two figures and to confirm the original relationship that he has established between David and God. Throughout the poem that relationship is reconfirmed by association, by direct assertion, and by the fallen characters' inversion of what the

narrator asserts to be the true order of things. Those recon-
firmations of David's relationship with God—especially the
increasing emphasis on David's kingly role—work to transform David from private father to public king.

With his first answer to the tempter, Absalom directly asserts the godlike nature of David's rule while revealing his
own character. Furthermore, Dryden makes clear the distinction between the divine order of David's rule, in which
Absalom can participate as long as he resists the temptation
to usurp David's power, and the satanic order that Achitophel
and the malcontents represent:

> And what Pretence have I
> To take up Arms for Publick Liberty?
> My Father Governs with unquestion'd Right;
> The Faiths Defender, and Mankinds Delight:
> Good, Gracious, Just, observant of the Laws;
> And Heav'n by Wonders has Espous'd his Cause.
>
> [315–20]

The portrait of David continues at some length, detailing the
king's mildness, humility, and mercy. Far from the weak, de-
bilitated king whom Achitophel describes, Absalom's portrait
asserts David's skill as a ruler, the divine sanction of his
reign, and his godlike qualities as king. But since those qualities are, at this point, christic rather than Jehovic, care must
be taken not to confuse mildness and humility with political
weakness. Together with the previous reference to David's
fatal mercy (l. 146), Absalom's description of David is a confirmation of the king's typological relationship to Christ.

However, gradual changes overcome Absalom as the desire
for greatness infects him. The first change occurs as he praises
David's generosity:

> What more can I expect while *David* lives,
> All but his Kingly Diadem he gives;
> And that: But there he Paus'd; then Sighing, said,
> Is Justly Destin'd for a Worthier Head.
>
> [345–48]

The "Kingly Diadem," symbol of royalty itself, ignites the fire of ambition in Absalom. He then capitulates even further to the desire to rule:

> Why am I Scanted by a Niggard Birth?
> My Soul Disclaims the Kindred of her Earth:
> And made for Empire, Whispers me within;
> Desire of Greatness is a Godlike Sin.
>
> [369–72]

And the narrator comments:

> Him Staggering so when Hells dire Agent found,
> While fainting Vertue scarce maintain'd her Ground.
>
> [373–74]

What was implicit is now explicit: Achitophel is "Hells dire Agent." The syntax, diction, and epithet—all conspicuously Miltonic—seal the identification of Achitophel with Satan.[20]

Having fully revealed the satanic and divine dimensions of Achitophel and David, and having charted Absalom's flight between the two, Dryden next turns to Achitophel's malcontents and David's allies. Though his method changes at this point, Dryden does not lose his grasp on either structure or theme.[21] Through the descriptions of the enemies and allies he extends the symbolic significance of the main characters by showing how other individuals in the poem participate in the typological identities of king and nation.

As in the initial presentation of Achitophel, Dryden's rendering of the malcontent Zimri makes the reader feel the anarchic dissipation of the character's energy and talent. Unlike David, whose energy is creative, Zimri scatters his energies without control. The well-known description of Zimri (ll. 543–68) suggests a character drawn from Milton's paradise of fools:

> All th' unaccomplisht works of Nature's hand,
> Abortive, monstrous, or unkindly mixt,
> Dissolv'd on Earth, fleet hither, and in vain,
> Till final dissolution, wander here.[22]

The moral significance of Milton's limbo can be felt in the description of Zimri, in the very cadence of Dryden's verse.

The other malcontents have pronounced satanic or fallen characteristics. Balaam, though gifted in prophecy, endeavors to curse God's people and plots with the Moabites against Israel (Num. 22–24); Nadab sins before God by kindling his censer with "strange fire" (Lev. 10:1); and Shimei, like Achitophel, is an active blasphemer of God. The Miltonic allusion to the Sons of Belial (l. 598), who have a "glorious Time" when Shimei is their magistrate, is further evidence of his allegiance to "Hell's dire Agent." In Numbers 16, Corah appears as the leader of the rebellion against Moses and Aaron, and he is coupled with Cain and Balaam in the Epistle of Jude as an example of those who "despise dominion, and speak evil of dignities" (Jude 8).

Dryden's handling of Corah, however, goes beyond accusing him of the biblical crime of rebellion:

> Yet, *Corah,* thou shalt from Oblivion pass;
> Erect thy self thou Monumental Brass:
> High as the Serpent of thy mettall made,
> While Nations stand secure beneath thy shade.
>
> [632–35]

The brass serpent was, of course, held up by Moses in the desert to cure the rebellious Israelites of the curse of serpents that an angry God had visited on them (Num. 21:9); thus it connotes healing powers. In the New Testament the healing qualities of the brass serpent are seen as a foreshadowing of Christ's restorative powers (John 3:14–15), making it a type of Christ. But Corah, like Absalom, is a false Messiah. The irony of juxtaposing the biblical rebel and the typological symbol is sharpened and directed against Dryden's Restoration Corah, Titus Oates, by allusions to contemporary events. Oates, as chief witness against the Popish Plot and the self-proclaimed savior of the nation, epitomizes the biblical rebel and false savior. That Corah rebelled against God's chosen priest in the Old Testament implies, of course, that Oates rebelled against God's anointed in English history. Furthermore, in bearing false witness Oates is identified with the serpent in Genesis: the phrase "Serpent of thy mettall" is a play on the meaning of *metal,* the brass of Moses' serpent, and *mettle,* the stuff from which a man is made.

Throughout *Absalom and Achitophel* the English-Israelite metaphor associates the English civil war with a rebellion against God; the interregnum with the Egyptian bondage; and the Restoration dissatisfactions with, and plots against, the Stuart monarchy with the Israelites' complaining, idol worshiping, and backsliding in their journey to the Promised Land. Thus the brass serpent alludes to the whole narrative from Numbers. The conspiratorial, rebellious mood of the English is then directly associated with the murmuring of the Israelites; and Corah, Absalom, Achitophel, and the malcontents become the plague of fiery serpents visited on the English. Indeed, that image recurs at the close of the poem, as David predicts the demise of the plot: "Against themselves their Witnesses will Swear, / Till Viper-like their Mother Plot they tear" (ll. 1012–13).

The portraits of David's allies directly confirm what the renderings of the king's enemies imply. David's small, faithful band—his "short File" (l. 817)—suggests the theme of the closing books of *Paradise Lost:* the few just against the many wicked.[23] Moreover, in biblical commentary David was a type of Christ in the similarity of his faithful band to Christ's apostles.[24] Dryden is perhaps alluding to that figural association through Barzillai, who, "In Exile with his Godlike Prince . . . Mourn'd; / For him he Suffer'd, and with him Return'd" (ll. 823–24). Like Christ's apostles, who had continued with him in his temptations (Luke 22:28), Barzillai has endured David's trials and suffered for him. Possibly, too, the reference to Adriel replacing David's disobedient son (ll. 880–81) is meant to suggest the apostle who replaces Judas (Acts 1:24–26).

The main thrust of the portraits, however, lies less in individual parallels than in the effect of David's allies as a whole. Since the portraits of the allies are a preparation for the king's speech, Dryden is careful to keep the verbal texture of this prelude fairly simple. A more brilliant preparation for David's speech could have made it anticlimactic. The comparative simplicity of the portraits of David's allies is also important thematically. The controlled, corporate unity of the king's worthies is a significant contrast to the malcontents. Not only are Zimri and Corah men whose frenzy and fanaticism make them misfits in the ordered society that the poem holds as an ideal, but the verbal impact of their portraits severs the individual characters from the poem as a whole.

The movement of David from person to office—the confirmation of the king's godlike authority—is fulfilled in the closing ninety lines of the poem. It is not only a movement to be followed by the reader as Dryden turns gradually from the personal to the official; it is also one confirmed by David as he weighs his course of action:

> Thus long have I, by native mercy sway'd,
> My wrongs dissembl'd, my revenge delay'd:
> So willing to forgive th' Offending Age,
> So much the Father did the King asswage.
>
> [939–42]

Having shown the ruinous effect that the plot portends, Dryden has David speak at long last to assert the divinity of his kingship. Three times in the short verse paragraph that precedes David's speech the narrator repeats the relationship that David as king bears to God (ll. 933–38). The speech itself reviews David's long-suffering patience, his clemency, the false accusations of the people, and the paternal love that he still has for his rebellious son. The inconclusive fate of Absalom suggests, as critics have pointed out, that the king is still willing to see Absalom realize his potential as David's son if Absalom will repent of his attempt to seize the throne and affirm the spiritual kingship of the true Messiah.[25]

The fate of the Israelites, however, is not left undecided; the king regrets the ineffectuality of his mild reign and declares that his people require not the dispensation of grace but the dispensation of law:

> Oh that my Power to Saving were confin'd:
> Why am I forc'd, like Heaven, against my mind,
> To make Examples of another Kind?
>
> [999–1001]

Here and in the lines that follow English politics take on the full moral weight of Old Testament history. The English Israelites require the dispensation of law and, furthermore, as Jews reject the dispensation of mercy. David-Charles must use his power not only to save but also, like Jehovah in the Old Testament and like Christ in Revelation, to judge and to destroy the wicked. The English are restored at the end of the poem, but restored under the law. David has the power through God to create a political Eden, but only when the people acknowledge the divinity of his kingship. David's words, like God's and Christ's, establish order and renew time.

The conclusion of *Absalom and Achitophel* suggests apocalypse, the "Series of new time" conveying the figural meaning of the perfect order of the New Jerusalem; but Dryden, hovering between the sacred past and the figural future, displays a growing awareness of the political, and thus, moral recalcitrance of the English Israelites. The conclusion is at once political and figural: Dryden invokes both the model of lawful order in the Old Jerusalem and the model of perfect order in the *figura* of the New Jerusalem. And the political meaning of England's Israelite identity is brought into focus. If the English persist in acting like unregenerate Jews, then the king must revert from mildness to severe justice:

> Law they require, let Law then shew her Face;
> They coud not be content to look on Grace.
>
> .   .   .   .
>
> For Lawfull Pow'r is still Superiour found,
> When long driven back, at length it stands the ground.
>
> .   .   .   .
>
> Once more the Godlike *David* was Restor'd,
> And willing Nations knew their Lawfull Lord.
>
> [1006–7; 1024–25; 1030–31]

The figural allusions and the Miltonic extensions of the basic metaphor are brought to completion in the form of a political prescription for the English nation. Yet the narrative from 2 Samuel, with its attendant meanings, also permits Dryden to write the sacred history of the English people—to shape contemporary events in a manner that allows the reader to see how the present day embodies the past and, through that association, comes itself to participate in an eternal repetition of the archetypal events that the Bible records. The biblical metaphor, the typological associations, and the contemporary political applications are all working to transform the Restoration present tense and the biblical past tense into a symbolic eternal tense.

5 FROM THE SACRED PAST TO A NEUTRAL PRESENT

The 1680s were an eventful but not altogether happy decade for Dryden the political poet and for the monarchy that he had celebrated and defended since 1660. Shaftesbury was imprisoned on the charge of high treason in July 1681, released by a London jury in November *(The Medall)*, and dead in Holland in 1683. The year 1685 saw the sudden death of Charles II *(Threnodia Augustalis)*, the coronation of his Roman Catholic brother, the execution of Monmouth, and Dryden's conversion to Catholicism. In 1687 Dryden published *The Hind and the Panther*, a lengthy apologia for his new religion; and in June 1688 Tonson issued Dryden's last official panegyric, *Britannia Rediviva*, a celebration of the birth of James II's son. William of Orange landed at Torbay in November 1688, and in December James fled to France. A convention parliament offered the crown to William and Mary in 1689; and Dryden, now a Roman Catholic, relinquished to Thomas Shadwell the offices of poet laureate and historiographer royal—a victory whose irony was undoubtedly savored by the dunce of *Mac Flecknoe*.

The connections that can be made between the personal and political fortunes of Dryden and the Stuarts during the 1680s, and the inferences that can be drawn from the coincidence of Dryden's conversion with James's ascent to the throne in 1685, have encouraged many to question Dryden's integrity and motives.[1] Yet the movement toward Catholicism is implicit in his political poetry of the 1680s and can be felt in the changing use to which he puts the complex of biblical metaphors found in the earlier political poetry. In the simplest terms, Dryden's conversion is a movement from faith in the nation as a covenanted people to faith in the body of the church as God's true Israel. During the 1680s the focus of

Dryden's poetry shifts from a Protestant reliance on politics as a redemptive instrument to a Catholic confession of faith in the unerring guide of an authoritative church—a belief, Dryden asserts in *The Hind and the Panther,* that insures the bliss of God's grace.[2]

The Medall, Threnodia Augustalis, and *Britannia Rediviva* illustrate how Dryden's use of sacred analogy and biblical metaphor narrows and how the reduction in the capacity of sacred history to accommodate the interaction of king and nation, especially in the two panegyrics, results in the abstraction of political issues. Gradually Dryden releases the nation from sacred metaphor, so that in *Threnodia Augustalis* and *Britannia Rediviva* the celebration of the monarch seems to be a return to the medieval Catholic celebration of the king as *typus Christi*[3]—a celebration that does not include the nation in the metaphors of sacred history. In Dryden's personal epistles and panegyrics of the late 1680s and 1690s, individuals claim the correlative relationship with the Old Testament elect that had earlier illuminated the trials and promises of the whole nation.

The Medall

The central identifications drawn from sacred history in *The Medall* (1682) are Shaftesbury as Satan and the English people as recalcitrant Jews—not the nation of God's promise but a people insistent on a false god. Both themes are familiar from *Absalom and Achitophel,* but both are developed in *The Medall* without the redemptive counterpart of a godlike king or an Edenic state. The identification of Shaftesbury with Satan begins not with the early reference to Lucifer (l. 21) but in the epigraph from the *Aeneid* (6. 588–89) that heads the introductory "Epistle To the Whigs": "Per Graiûm populos, mediaequae per Elidis Urbem / Ibat ovans; Divumque sibi poscebat Honores." At this point in his underworld journey Aeneas has passed from the Aloean twins, who "dar'd in Fight the Thund'rer to defy," to Salmoneus, another rebel against the gods and, moreover, an aspirant to a false godhood. Aeneas finds him "suff'ring cruel Pains . . . / For emulating *Jove*." [4] Thus Dryden's epigraph introduces one of the poem's central motifs in pointing to the relationship between Salmoneus (Shaftesbury) and Satan.

The Medall begins with Dryden interpreting for his audience the meaning of the Whig medallion struck to celebrate Shaftesbury's release from the Tower of London. The medallion, an icon for the seditious Whigs, represents a false king and a counterfeit god; Shaftesbury is characterized as a "Monster" (l. 4), an "Idol" (l. 7), and the counterpart of *"Lucifer"* (l. 21). As the prophets of the Old Testament proclaimed the Word of God, as the psalmist rejoiced in his Lord, so the London Whig pronounces "the Word" for the false lord; Shaftesbury and his people are perversions of God and his prophets:

> The Word, pronounc'd aloud by Shrieval voice,
> *Laetamur*, which, in *Polish*, is *rejoyce*.
> The Day, Month, Year, to the great Act are join'd:
> And a new Canting Holiday design'd.
>
> [14–17]

In the biblical sense, the Word embraces creative and prophetic meanings: God's Word creates the world; the Word made flesh redeems mankind; and God's prophets preach the Word in both the Old and the New Testaments. By ironically linking the creation of the medal with the biblical notion of rejoicing in the Word, Dryden establishes at the beginning of the poem the terms in which the political issues are to be understood. Instead of spreading light and order, Shaftesbury's priests spread the disease of his political ideas:

> But what thou giv'st, that Venom still remains;
> And the pox'd Nation feels Thee in their Brains.
> What else inspires the Tongues, and swells the Breasts
> Of all thy bellowing Renegado Priests,
> That preach up Thee for God; dispence thy Laws;
> And with thy Stumm ferment their fainting Cause?
>
> [265–70]

Shaftesbury is not simply an enemy of Royalist political principles, he is the inversion of order. His satanic identity, suggested in the epigraph, is developed early in the poem:

> Five daies he sate, for every cast and look;
> Four more than God to finish *Adam* took.
> But who can tell what Essence Angels are,
> Or how long Heav'n was making *Lucifer?*
>
> [18–21]

The theme of Shaftesbury as Satan, infecting the nation and seducing the multitude, is woven through the poem. Shifting between the present and the past, between the particular occasion of the poem and references to sacred history, Dryden creates in Shaftesbury a figure who embodies the archfiend. Central to the various representations of Shaftesbury is the figure of Satan as the deformed seducer of *Paradise Lost;* and as Milton created from physical attributes a metaphor for the fallen angel's spiritual state, so Dryden seizes on Shaftesbury's bodily defects as an expression of his spiritual condition. Deformed, of pygmy size, he is the "Vermin, wriggling in th' Usurper's Ear" (l. 31), Delilah betraying English "native Strength" (l. 72), the "Fiend confess'd, without a vaile" (l. 81), Jehu spurring the "hot mouth'd" populace to rebellion (l. 119), and the "Pander of the Peoples hearts," "Crooked" and "Serpentine" in his ways (ll. 256–57). By repeating those characteristic words and phrases, Dryden transforms the analogy between Shaftesbury and Lucifer into sacred metaphor.

The identification of Shaftesbury with Satan is one part of the scriptural frame of *The Medall;* a second is the familiar identification of the English people with the Israelite nation. Although Dryden does not often invoke the relationship, it significantly extends the political meaning of Shaftesbury's satanic identity and serves to indicate Dryden's changing use of the metaphor. In Dryden's earlier identifications of the English with the Israelites there is a suggestion of backsliding, idol worshipping, and disobedience; but the emphasis in the early years of the Restoration is clearly on the promise of the covenanted people. *Astraea Redux, To His Sacred Majesty,* and *Annus Mirabilis* all close with visions of an impending golden age and prophesies of a paradise regained. However, in his political poetry of the 1680s Dryden is more sharply aware of the presence of Satan in the Eden that the English were to enjoy with the restoration of the anointed king. In *Absalom and Achitophel,* but even more so in *The Medall,* the tendency to sin, the backsliding of the Old Testament nation, becomes not simply an expression of England's reluctance to live peaceably with the Stuart monarchy but an expression of all men's reluctance to be saved. There is in *The Medall* a darkening of Dryden's political optimism, of his trust in the ability of the nation to be reclaimed. The English experience is cast as a recapitulation of the Israelite experience, both pointing to that continual rebellion and fall that will recur as long as man lives in the unregenerate state. As Dryden generalizes political occasion and historical example into moral conditions, religion, not politics, becomes the instrument of redemption; if not the nation, then perhaps the individual soul can be reclaimed.

The references in *The Medall* to the factious English as "Ideots" (l. 2), the "Crowd" (l. 82), a "Beast" (l. 120), and a Cyclops (l. 226) look forward to the way in which Dryden will characterize the nation in *Threnodia Augustalis* and *Britannia Rediviva,* as does his portrayal of the nation as murmuring Israelites:

> Too happy *England,* if our good we knew;
> Wou'd we possess the freedom we pursue!
> The lavish Government can give no more:
> Yet we repine; and plenty makes us poor.
> God try'd us once; our Rebel-fathers fought;
> He glutted 'em with all the pow'r they sought:
> Till, master'd by their own usurping Brave,
> The free-born Subject sunk into a Slave.
> We loath our Manna, and we long for Quails;
> Ah, what is man, when his own wish prevails!
> How rash, how swift to plunge himself in ill;
> Proud of his Pow'r, and boundless in his Will!

[123–34]

The language and ideas echo Dryden's brief prologue to *The Unhappy Favourite* (1682):

> Tell me you Powers, why should vain Man pursue,
> With endless Toyl, each object that is new,
> And for the seeming substance leave the true—
> Why should he quit for hopes his certain good,
> And loath the Manna of his dayly food?
> Must *England* still the Scene of Changes be,
> Tost and Tempestuous like our Ambient Sea?
>
> .   .   .   .
>
> Our Land's an *Eden,* and the Main's our Fence,
> While we Preserve our State of Innocence.
>
> [13–19, 27–28]

In *The Medall,* however, there is no Eden to return to, no state of innocence that the English yet might win. England is no longer the Promised Land:

> Of *Israel's* Tribes thou hast a numerous band;
> But still the *Canaanite* is in the Land.
>
> [177–78]

The civil war was the Fall, and the English as Israelites persist in rejecting God's gift of manna.

In *To His Sacred Majesty* Dryden used the biblical manna as a metaphor for the coronation of the king: the crowning of Charles II, like the heavenly manna, was a sign of God's watchfulness over his people, an instrument for their preservation. But in *The Medall* the English reject the manna of their present government and long for the "Quails" of usurping power. The story of the Israelites who longed for quail is told in Numbers 11. Dissatisfied with the manna that God had granted them for their sustenance, the Israelites longed for the flesh and spices of Egypt. The relationship between the lust for flesh and Egyptian bondage is important for Dryden's polemical purposes in *The Medall.* As the Israelites would willingly lose their freedom and forego the worship of their true God to satisfy the appetites of the flesh, so the En-

glish lust after usurping freedom and long to return to the
Egyptian bondage of the interregnum years. Moreover, the
whole episode from Exodus carries the moral weight of the
familiar patristic exegesis of the Israelites' departure from
Egypt.[5] Not only was Egyptian bondage physical servitude, it
was also spiritual slavery; and surely something of that slavery
is attributed by Dryden to those who long for the past of the
Commonwealth years. The Stuart monarchy is "our good"
and the "freedom we pursue," while the Commonwealth
usurpers were "Rebel-fathers" and the "free-born Subject
sunk into a Slave." [6]

England as backsliding Israel informs both the Old and
New Testament references and allusions. The idol worshiping at the beginning of the poem (l. 7) and the melting of the
king (l. 228) repeat the Israelites' casting of the molten calf;
and the New Testament parable of the wicked husbandmen
(Matt. 21:33–46) suggests, in the context of sacred history, not
only Restoration politics but also Israel's rejection of Christ:

> If Sovereign Right by Sovereign Pow'r they scan,
> The same bold Maxime holds in God and Man:
> God were not safe, his Thunder cou'd they shun
> He shou'd be forc'd to crown another Son.
> Thus, when the Heir was from the Vineyard thrown,
> The rich Possession was the Murth'rers own.
>
> [214–19]

Charles is analogous to God, and the Whigs as Jews reject the
legitimate heir—the parable moves neatly between English
and Jewish history.[7]

As in *Absalom and Achitophel,* scriptural history is a frame
in which the satirist can set the vices, ignorance, and errors
of the nation; but unlike *Absalom and Achitophel, The
Medall* focuses relentlessly on those characters and episodes
from the Old Testament that confirm the seduction, rebellion, and fall in Eden. As a result, Dryden seems to echo Moses
upbraiding the Israelites in Deuteronomy 9:6–7: "Understand therefore, that the Lord thy God giveth thee not this
good land to possess it for thy righteousness; for thou art a

stiffnecked people. Remember, and forget not, how thou pro-
vokedst the Lord thy God to wrath in the wilderness: from
the day that thou didst depart out of the land of Egypt, until
ye came unto this place, ye have been rebellious against the
Lord." The concluding verse paragraph of *The Medall*, with
its promise of "our wild Labours, wearied into Rest," is
hardly the realization of any redemptive motif developed in
the poem but, rather, a dimly hopeful look toward the future.
Dryden has come far indeed from the renewal of time at the
close of *Astraea Redux* or the apocalyptic fire in *Annus Mirabilis;* the events in the remaining years of the Stuart monarchy did little to renew his earlier belief in political redemption.

Threnodia Augustalis and *Britannia Rediviva*

Threnodia Augustalis and *Britannia Rediviva* complete Dryden's attempt to record the sacred history of the English nation. A comparison of *Threnodia Augustalis* and *Britannia
Rediviva* with the Restoration panegyrics reveals in Dryden's
last official poems considerably more emphasis on the divinity
of the king and a marked reluctance to involve the English
nation in the process of redemptive history. In neither *Threnodia Augustalis* nor *Britannia Rediviva* are the English people able to participate in the renewal and restoration that
Dryden had prophesied so often in the past. The diminution
of the metaphor is noticeable both in Dryden's isolating the
divinely sanctified monarch from the life of the nation and
in his substituting abstractions like "Faction," "Domestick
Treachery," "th' ungrateful Rout," and "Godless men" for
the English people's earlier identity as a blessed if recalcitrant
nation. Both characteristics suggest a growing rigidity in Dryden's handling of political issues—a loss of the ability so sup-
plely and powerfully demonstrated in *Absalom and Achitophel* to see nation and king unified in terms of sacred
metaphor.

Threnodia Augustalis (1685) begins not in the Edenic state nor in the past of Jewish history but with a reminiscence of the classical golden age:

> We liv'd as unconcern'd and happily
> As the first Age in Natures golden Scene;
> Supine amidst our flowing Store,
> We slept securely, and we dream't of more.
>
> [12-15]

The choice of the golden age as an expression of political security and harmony does not in itself signal a change in Dryden's handling of the relationship of English history to the past. Indeed, the phrasing closely parallels a couplet near the beginning of *To His Sacred Majesty*: "We had not yet exhausted all our store / When you refresh'd our joyes by adding more" (ll. 21-22). What does mark a change and what points to a retreat from the tensions of contemporary affairs is the fact that the image of the golden age is simply posited at the beginning of the poem and is not involved in the expression of either the immediate past of English political life or of an ideal toward which the nation should strive. It is an undeveloped fiction that is contradicted by what Dryden says of the reign of Charles II:

> Through Hazzards numberless and great,
> Thou hast deriv'd this mighty Blessing down,
> And fixt the fairest Gemm that decks th' Imperial Crown:
> Not Faction, when it shook thy Regal Seat,
> Not Senates, insolently loud,
> (Those Ecchoes of a thoughtless Croud)
> Not Foreign or Domestick Treachery,
> Could warp thy Soul to their Unjust Decree.
>
> [315-22]

It is also striking that Dryden renders the enemies of the crown in abstract terms throughout the poem. Charles forgives the guilt and crimes of "Godless men, and of Rebellious times" (l. 264) and saves the sinking ship of state:

When Faction like a Tempest rose,
In Death's most hideous form,
Then, Art to Rage thou didst oppose,
To weather out the Storm:
Not quitting thy Supream command,
Thou heldst the Rudder with a steady hand,
Till safely on the Shore the Bark did land:
The Bark that all our Blessings brought,
Charg'd with thy Self and *James,* a doubly Royal fraught.

[390–98]

This "Bark" is not, as in *To His Sacred Majesty,* also the ark of redemptive history, for Dryden no longer conceives of the English as the remnant but, rather, as "Faction like a Tempest"—not a blessed people, but a storm. The king's foes are no longer named, nor are they given an identity that involves them, through analogy or typology, with the past:

The Best, and best belov'd of Kings,
And best deserving to be so,
When scarce he had escap'd the fatal blow
Of Faction and Conspiracy,
Death did his promis'd hopes destroy.

[404–8]

"Faction," "thoughtless Croud," "Domestick Treachery"— such images are neither given the individual identity of characters, as in *Absalom and Achitophel* and *The Medall,* nor are they metaphorically related to the sacred past. They are simply abstractions that oppose the crown and the harmony for which it stands.

Against the thin and abstract rendering of the factious crowd Dryden sets a richly detailed portrait of the king as divine monarch—as *typus Christi.* Charles is "God's Image, God's Anointed" (l. 63), the "New-born Phoenix" (l. 364), and "That all forgiving King, / The type of him above, / That inexhausted spring / Of clemency and Love" (ll. 257–60). His reign is an expression of Providence: "New Miracles approach'd th' Etherial Throne, / Such as his wondrous Life had oft and lately known" (ll. 90–91); "For all those Joys thy Restauration brought, / For all the Miracles it wrought" (ll. 292–93). Like David, Charles is a monarch after God's own heart, yet Charles is even more serene and merciful than the biblical king. And like Hezekiah, who, in his miraculous recovery from death (2 Kings 20), was frequently read as a type of Christ,[8] Charles is also reprieved from death.

As Charles's brother, James is an expression of piety and devotion (ll. 36–40; 248–56); as the new king, he is a hero cast in "Heaven's peculiar Mold" (l. 432)—Alcides (Hercules) subduing the hissing snakes:

> View then a *Monarch* ripen'd for a Throne.
> *Alcides* thus his race began,
> O're Infancy he swiftly ran;
> The future God, at first was more than Man:
> Dangers and Toils, and *Juno*'s Hate
> Even o're his Cradle lay in wait;
> And there he grappled first with Fate:
> In his young Hands the hissing Snakes he prest,
> So early was the Deity confest;
> Thus, by degrees, he rose to *Jove*'s Imperial Seat;
> Thus difficulties prove a Soul *legitimately* great.
> Like his, our Hero's Infancy was try'd;
> Betimes the Furies did their Snakes provide;
> And, to his Infant Arms oppose
> His Father's Rebels, and his Brother's Foes;
> The more opprest the higher still he rose:
> Those were the Preludes of his Fate,
> That form'd his Manhood, to subdue
> The *Hydra* of the many-headed, hissing Crew.
>
> [446–64]

Not only was the image of Alcides strangling the snakes a frequently cited pagan foreshadowing of Christ's victory over Satan, but the direct reference to James subduing the "hissing Crew"—echoing Milton's characterization of the fallen angels turned to serpents in hell (*Paradise Lost* 10. 504–23)—suggests Christ's victory over the devil and all demonic powers.

Yet for all its typological detail, *Threnodia Augustalis* fails
to make a case for the king as an expression of divine monarchy in the political life of the English nation. Like David
and Christ, Charles and James are redemptive kings, but in
the design of the poem Dryden fails to allow for redemptive
action. Although the poem concludes with a prophecy, it is
drawn exclusively from classical literature and not, as in the
past, from sacred history or classical literature combined with
biblical apocalypse:

> For once, O Heav'n, unfold thy Adamantine Book;
> And let his wondring *Senate* see,
> If not thy firm Immutable Decree,
> At least the second Page, of strong contingency;
> Such as consists with wills, Originally free:
>> Let them, with glad amazement, look
>> On what their happiness may be:
> Let them not still be obstinately blind,
> Still to divert the Good thou hast design'd,
> Or with Malignant penury,
> To sterve the Royal Vertues of his Mind.
> Faith is a Christian's and a Subject's Test,
> Oh give them to believe, and they are surely blest!
>> They do; and, with a distant view, I see
>> Th' amended Vows of *English* Loyalty.
> And all beyond that Object, there appears
> The long Retinue of a Prosperous Raign.
>
> [491–507]

The poem closes as Dryden enumerates the signs of a prosper-
ous reign for James. But Dryden's belief in the possibility of
political redemption is faltering. "For once," "Let them . . .
look," "Let them not still be . . . blind," "Oh give them to believe"—these are subjunctive petitions bordering on a despair
of realizing such a wish. And, indeed, the emphasis on faith
and belief seems to be another signal that Dryden is turning
away from English political life as an area that can respond to
the promise that God recorded in Israelite history. Furthermore, Dryden's shift from prayer to vision is unconvincing

(ll. 503–4), for there has been nothing in the poem to suggest that "They do" believe. Dryden's vision seems to be no vision at all, but a weary repetition of the props of a political fortune in which he seems no longer to believe.

The poet laureate, however, was called on once more to revive that belief in the fortunes of the Stuart monarchy. With the birth of a son to James II, supporters of the king no doubt saw new promise for the Stuarts, and Dryden joined them in celebrating the prince's birth. *Britannia Rediviva* (1688), Dryden's poem on the occasion, is in some ways more coherent than *Threnodia Augustalis*, but like the earlier panegyric it fails to achieve a convincing reading of contemporary events as an expression of sacred history. There are two brief references to the English as Israelites (ll. 66, 285), but both, like the passage in *Threnodia Augustalis* on the murmuring English (ll. 425–28), stress Israel as a backsliding nation; Dryden makes no reference to the redemptive potential of Israel as a whole. As in *Threnodia Augustalis*, Dryden makes a clear distinction between the divinity of the king and prince and the condition of the nation. The birth of James II's son is marked by a "Brighter Sun" (l. 9), and the infant bears the image of the Trinity:

> Or did the Mighty Trinity conspire,
> As once, in Council to Create our Sire?
> It seems as if they sent the New-Born Guest
> To wait on the Procession of their Feast;
> And on their Sacred Anniverse decree'd
> To stamp their Image on the promis'd Seed.
> Three Realms united, and on One bestow'd,
> An Emblem of their Mystick Union show'd:
> The Mighty Trine the Triple Empire shar'd,
> As every Person wou'd have One to guard.
>
> [25–34]

The divinity of the prince is suggested through images traditionally associated with the first and second Adam ("An Emblem of their Mystick Union," "our Sire," "the promis'd Seed") and advanced as Dryden casts the prince in opposition to the "Dragon" of the Commonwealth party:

> Our wants exact at least that moderate stay:
> For see the Dragon winged on his way,
> To watch the Travail, and devour the Prey.
>
> [51-53]

According to Dryden's own notes to the poem, the Commonwealth party is to be identified with the dragon in Revelation 12:3-4, and the birth of the prince is to be identified with the birth of the child in Revelation 12:2, whom the dragon has come to devour. In the general context of Revelation, this episode is a prediction of the defeat of Antichrist and the millennial rule of Christ on earth.

Dryden presses the identification of the prince with Christ even further, in spite of his disclaimer (l. 54), with a reference to Alcides' defeat of the besieging serpents:

> Or, if Allusions may not rise so high,
> Thus, when *Alcides* rais'd his Infant Cry,
> The Snakes besieg'd his Young Divinity:
> But vainly with their forked Tongues they threat;
> For Opposition makes a Heroe Great.
> To needful Succour all the Good will run;
> And *Jove* assert the Godhead of his Son.
>
> [54-60]

As in *Threnodia Augustalis* (ll. 457-64), the reference to Alcides strangling the snakes can be read as an allusion to Christ's victory over Satan. Combined with the reference to Revelation, the pagan myth supports the identification of the prince and Christ.[9]

Yet for all the interesting detail that Dryden uses to suggest the divinity of the prince, the relationship between the prospective king and the country—between the crown and its enemies—remains very abstract. The political opponents of the Stuarts are named and identified with Satan, but the meaning of that identification is not worked out in either dramatic or metaphoric terms. Rather, the confrontation between the prince and the Commonwealth party occurs on the plane of allegorical fantasy. Occasionally, however, a biblical reference is extended to contemporary events, and at those points Dryden's language seems freshest and most forceful in its use of detail. In one such passage Dryden returns to 2 Samuel, using the story of David at Araunah's threshing floor to parallel James's support of the Roman Catholic Church. The troubled spring of 1688 suggests Israel visited by pestilence and death after David's sin of numbering Israel; and James taking part in the Roman Catholic rites repeats David's sacrifice:

> Enough already has the Year foreslow'd
> His wonted Course, the Seas have overflow'd,
> The Meads were floated with a weeping Spring,
> And frighten'd birds in Woods forgot to sing;
> The Strong-limb'd Steed beneath his harness faints,
> And the same shiv'ring sweat his Lord attaints.
> When will the Minister of Wrath give o're?
> Behold him; at *Araunah*'s threshing-floor.
> He stops, and seems to sheath his flaming brand;
> Pleas'd with burnt Incense, from our *David*'s hand.
> *David* has bought the *Jebusites* abode,
> And rais'd an Altar to the Living God.
>
> [169–80]

David's offering foreshadows Christ's sacrifice, and the altar stands for the true temple, where expiatory sacrifice is offered in succeeding generations.[10] Thus the newborn prince, through his presence in the land and especially in his baptism, atones for the sins of the people ("Let his Baptismal Drops for us attone; / Lustrations for Offences not his own" [ll. 188–89]). And David's Jebusite abode is the Catholic Church, which James II had embraced and in which succeeding generations can take Communion, the symbol of Christ's sacrifice. The biblical allusion works on both a figural and a historical level; the specific details of Restoration history are read in terms of biblical history, and both are illuminated by the figural meaning that was given to Old Testament narrative.

But as a whole Dryden's poem on the birth of the prince does not work toward an interpretation of contemporary events through biblical allusion and typological analogy. Years before, Dryden had spoken of the role of the poet as prophet in *To my Honored Friend, Sir Robert Howard* (1660):

> But to write worthy things of worthy men
> Is the peculiar talent of your Pen:
> Yet let me take your Mantle up, and I
> Will venture in your right to prophesy.
>
> [99–102]

In *Britannia Rediviva* Dryden very consciously resigns the prophetic office in which he had so often performed: "Poets are not Prophets, to foreknow / What Plants will take the Blite, and what will grow" (ll. 71–72). And the ending of the poem, which is usually Dryden's occasion to recapitulate the meaning of English history in redemptive terms, is noticeably secular in *Britannia Rediviva*. Although he refers to the heavenly attributes of the just king, the closing couplet and triplet refer not to the sacred past or to the apocalyptic future but to the neutral present:

> Life and State
> Are One to Fortune subject, One to Fate:
> Equal to all, you justly frown or smile,
> Nor Hopes, nor Fears your steady Hand beguile;
> Your self our Ballance hold, the Worlds, our Isle.
>
> [357–61]

These lines, Dryden's last as poet laureate, seem a world apart from the English Israel of the Restoration panegyrics or of *Absalom and Achitophel;* but that English Israel was the product of a special conjunction of political, literary, and religious ideas. By 1688 not only had the political and religious climate changed but the poet himself was a different man.

CONCLUSION

In 1924 Bonamy Dobrée wrote of Dryden, "The truth is he was not much interested in life, he cared nothing for politics, and probably not much for religion." [1] Over the past fifty years students of Dryden have come to hold a different opinion about the depth and seriousness of his concern with politics and religion. Dryden has been so often cast as the herald of English neoclassicism that it has taken a special effort to understand him as a seventeenth-century poet writing not so much in the shadow of Pope as in the company of Milton and Marvell. Dryden was very conscious of the ways in which he was not an Elizabethan; but, perhaps more than he was willing to acknowledge in his role as apologist for the new drama, he owed debts very similar to those of his contemporaries to the literary and intellectual past.

While it is not difficult to assume that contemporaries of Donne and Herbert could see the figural perspective in public lives and political acts, literary historians have so often insisted on the radical transformation of post-Restoration culture that students of the period have been cautious in assuming the continuity of certain traditions throughout the century. However, critics who point out the cynical and libertine elements of Restoration literature cannot disallow the influence that such traditions as Renaissance figuralism continued to exert on the devotional and political language of poets, divines, and pamphleteers during the latter part of the seventeenth century. Indeed, the libertine attitudes of Donne's love poetry and the intensely religious, figural imagination of his sermons affirm that such disparate elements existed side by side in a single mind as well as in an age.

To place Dryden within this seventeenth-century context is to illuminate an important aspect of his career as a poet and as an apologist for the Stuart monarchy. The Restoration panegyrics are Dryden's first essays in the sacred history of English political life, but they are not the works of a poet unfamiliar with the language of sacred history. The sureness with which Dryden invokes the figural perspective suggests that he is relying on a well-known and widely understood set of assumptions: the monarch as divinely anointed sovereign performs saving and restoring acts in the convenanted history of a blessed though recalcitrant nation. The panegyrics display an easy congruence between the sacred past and prophetic future.

In *Annus Mirabilis* Dryden applies scriptural history to contemporary events with a greater awareness of its apologetic and polemical edge, arguing through figural analogy for the christic identity of the king and the efficacy of his sacrificial acts in preserving the life and assuring the bounty of the nation. Recording the direct threat of rebellion, *Absalom and Achitophel* extends the metaphor to its most complex and sophisticated form. As the threats to political order and stability increased, so, up to a point, did the vigor and imagination with which Dryden was able to respond through the terms of sacred history. The subtlety and facility with which Dryden suggests the archetypal patterns implicit in the political situation of the poem while applying with great particularity the sacred identity of the blessed and damned elements of Anglo-Judaic Israel demonstrate how the deepening political problems of the early 1680s engaged Dryden's fullest response to the political potential of sacred metaphor.

But the ability of the metaphor to bridge the widening gap between political realities and political hopes diminshed steadily, as did the political viability of the Stuart monarchy. *The Medall* pursues with satiric energy and abrasiveness the theme of political recalcitrance that is part of the subject matter of *Absalom and Achitophel,* but it does so without the relief of a redemptive counterpart—a godlike king. In *Threnodia Augustalis* and *Britannia Rediviva* Dryden can no longer conceive of the symbols of divine monarch and elect nation as an imaginative whole. In his last political poems

England is Israel only as a backsliding and sinful people, and more often than that the nation is simply an ungrateful rout, an unruly mob threatening the divinely sanctified monarch.

The political poetry, when seen in terms of a metaphoric presentation of sacred history, suggests a rising and falling belief in the possibility of political redemption that parallels Dryden's changing religious attitudes during this period—attitudes that are publicly marked by his conversion to Roman Catholicism in 1685. As the poet turned away from the possibility of national election, he was drawn to the possibility of individual grace. Israel, so long the metaphor for the English nation, becomes at the opening of *The Hind and the Panther* the metaphoric identity of the Roman Catholic Church; and in the panegyrics of the poet's later years the lives of such individuals as the countess of Abingdon and the duchess of Ormond, rather than the English nation, express the grace of God's providence. Dryden's movement from social and political problems to devotional argument and celebration—his attraction to the authority and dogma of the Roman Catholic Church—is an interesting parallel to the career of T. S. Eliot. For Eliot, as well as Dryden, public life was finally susceptible to correction only to a limited degree.

Dryden's long engagement with sacred history is an illuminating perspective from which to consider his personal and poetic development; perhaps, too, the individual career affords some insight into the broader problem of relating national mythology, historical events, and political poetry. It is more than coincidence that Dryden's political muse faltered at the moment the fortunes of the Stuarts were thrust on the unlikely heir of Charles II's throne, James II. But it is not only Dryden's poetry that illustrates the elusive and complex relationship between the aesthetic success of political poetry and the viability of public figures. The glorification of Elizabeth after the defeat of the Spanish Armada, Marvell's celebration of Cromwell in *The First Anniversary*, like Dryden's exaltation of Charles II in a poem such as *Absalom and Achitophel*, depend on the coincidence of language, belief, and political realities—a complex knot whose tying is the special talent of political poetry. The political poet is more dependent than most artists on the coincidence of variables, for he must not only look to his heart and write but must also keep his finger on the national pulse, disclose the failures of the opposition, and carefully bolster the image of his sometimes difficult hero. Perhaps it is just this act of holding in tension the many variables of his material that accounts for the peculiar strength and attraction of the successful political poet, the craftsman who triumphs over partisan stances and fading events through the enduring monument of his art.

NOTES
INDEX

NOTES

CHAPTER 1

1. Another example is provided by Howard Schless's gloss on line 119 of *The Medall* in George de F. Lord et al., eds., *Poems on Affairs of State* (New Haven, 1963–), 3:51, ed. Schless (1968). The line reads: "But this new *Jehu* spurs the hot mouth'd horse"; Schless glosses the line: "*Jehu:* Cf. 2 Kings 9:20. Jehu became the type of headlong revolutionary who loosed bestial forces (usually, the mob) which he could not fully control."

2. See, e.g., the review of Rachel Trickett's *The Honest Muse* in the *Times Literary Supplement*, 24 October 1968, p. 1202, in which the reviewer uses the term *type-figure,* or the review of Mark Boulby's *Herman Hesse: His Mind and Art* by Theodore Ziolkowski in *Modern Language Quarterly* 29 (1968):373. Mr. Ziolkowski uses *typology* in the following manner: "First, he has isolated what might be called a basic typological pattern underlying many of Hesse's stories and novels: the enclosed circle from which the hero breaks out, only to return at the end."

3. See Sheila Ralphs's review of A. C. Charity's *Events and Their Afterlife* in *Medium Aevum* 37 (1968):93–95.

4. This subject has received general treatment in H. R. MacCallum, "Milton and Figurative Interpretation of the Bible," *University of Toronto Quarterly* 31 (1962):397–415; Barbara K. Lewalski, *Milton's Brief Epic* (Providence, 1966), pp. 164–76; Earl Miner, *Dryden's Poetry* (Bloomington, Ind., 1967), pp. 152–60; William G. Madsen, *From Shadowy Types to Truth* (New Haven, 1968), introduction, chap. 2 passim; and, most recently, Earl Miner's review of Milton scholarship, "Plundering the Egyptians; or, What We Learn from Recent Books on Milton," *Eighteenth-Century Studies* 3 (1969):296–305. Although each critic explores the nature and extent of figural interpretation of the Old Testament in the seventeenth century for different reasons, all demonstrate that the knowledge and practice of typological exegesis was very extensive. Madsen, for example, states: "Typological interpretation of the Old Testament was universally practiced by both Protestants and Catholics in Milton's day" (p. 3). My own attempt to demonstrate the widespread knowledge and use of typological interpretation will not recapitulate the findings already available but, rather, will approach the subject through the numerous typology manuals published during the seventeenth century, a source of typological exegesis not yet fully treated in the literature dealing with this question.

5. On the distinction between the Christian and christological approach to the Old Testament, see James Barr, *Old and New in Interpretation: A Study of the Two Testaments* (London, 1966), chap. 2.

6. On the background of covenant theology in the Reformed churches of the seventeenth century, see Charles S. McCoy, "Johannes Cocceius: Federal Theologian," *Scottish Journal of Theology* 16 (1963):352–70. J. L. Scott, in "The Covenant in the Theology of Karl Barth," *Scottish Journal of Theology* 17 (1964):182–98, has some interesting remarks on Cocceius and the scriptural sources of covenant theology.

7. See Barbara K. Lewalski, "*Samson Agonistes* and the 'Tragedy' of the Apocalypse," *PMLA* 85 (1970):1050–62.

8. See, e. g., K. J. Woollcombe, "The Biblical Origins and Patristic Development of Typology," in G. W. H. Lampe and Woollcombe, *Essays on Typology* (London, 1957), p. 39.

9. *Scenes from the Drama of European Literature* (New York, 1959), p. 53.

10. On the Old Testament origins of typology, see Horace D. Hummel, "The Old Testament Basis of Typological Interpretation," *Biblical Research* 9 (1964):38–50. David Daube, in *The Exodus Pattern in the Bible* (London, 1963), discusses the prototypical character of the exodus motif in Scripture, making some interesting suggestions for the Old Testament basis of typology in the Gospels. On the etymology of *figura*, see Auerbach, *Scenes*, p. 11. A discussion of the history of the word *type* can be found in Woollcombe and in Joseph A. Galdon, "Typology and Seventeenth-Century Literature" (Ph.D. diss., Columbia University, 1965), chap. 1.

11. All references to the Bible, unless otherwise indicated, are to the King James Version.

12. The bibliography of the history of exegetical traditions is extensive. Three basic works are Jean Daniélou, *From Shadows to Reality: Studies in the Biblical Typology of the Fathers,* trans. W. Hilberd (Westminster, Md., 1960); Henri de Lubac, *Exégèse médiévale: les quatre sens de l'Écriture,* 4 vols. (Paris, 1959–64); and Beryl Smalley, *The Study of the Bible in the Middle Ages,* 2d ed. (Oxford, 1952).

13. Sacvan Bercovitch, in *Horologicals to Chronometricals: The Rhetoric of the Jeremiad,* Literary Monographs, vol. 3 (Madison, 1970), treats the relationship between the exegetical and eschatological views of Augustine and the early Calvinists.

14. See Robert W. Hanning, *The Vision of History in Early Britain* (New York, 1966), pp. 22–43. The recent study by Marjorie Reeves, *The Influence of Prophecy in the Later Middle Ages: A Study of Joachimism* (Oxford, 1969), does much to illuminate the political uses of Scripture and prophecy in the later Middle Ages.

15. Bercovitch, *Horologicals to Chronometricals,* p. 16.

16. Hanning, *Vision of History in Early Britain,* p. 36. On Augustine's theory of history, see Theodor E. Mommsen, "St. Augustine and the Christian Idea of Progress: The Background of *The City of God,*" *Journal of the History of Ideas* 12 (1951):346–74.

17. I introduce the notion of correlative typology at this point in

order to describe the manner in which many seventeenth-century poets and divines saw the figural meaning of Old Testament narrative embodied in contemporary figures and events. Barbara K. Lewalski, in "*Samson Agonistes* and the 'Tragedy' of the Apocalypse," discusses this phenomenon and uses *correlative type* to describe the political application of Old Testament materials: "In the political sphere, the Old Testament and Christian personages relate as correlative types rather than as type and antitype, if the antitype is understood as, in some degree at least, a more perfect recapitulation and fulfillment of the type" (p. 1056). Murray Roston, whom Lewalski cites, uses the term *postfiguration* in discussing a similar phenomenon in biblical drama (*Biblical Drama in England* [Evanston, Ill., 1968], pp. 69–78).

18. *The Figures or Types of the Old Testament* (Dublin, 1683); *Moses unveiled; or, those figures which served unto the patterne and shaddow of heavenly things . . . briefly explained* (London, 1658); *The Mystical Brasen Serpent: with the Magnetical Vertue thereof* (London, 1653).

19. The information is gathered from the *Dictionary of National Biography*, s.v. "Mather, Samuel," "Guild, William," "Brinsley, John."

20. Mather, *Figures or Types*, sig. K1v.

21. Ibid., sig. K2.

22. Ibid.

23. Guild, *Moses unveiled*, sigs. A3–A4.

24. Brinsley, *Mystical Brasen Serpent*, sigs. B2–B2v.

25. *Figures or Types*, sig. 4R2.

26. Ibid., sigs. N1v–O1v.

27. All published in London. Some notion of the variety of theological stances among the commentators can be gained from the biographical information on these figures in the *DNB*.

28. For a representative listing of Renaissance typological commentary, see Sacvan Bercovitch, "Selective Check-List on Typology," *Early American Literature* 5, pt. 2 (1970):16–28.

29. Origen is mentioned in *Absalom and Achitophel* in the preface, "To the Reader." The suggestion that Dryden might have owned a copy of Peter of Lombard's *Expositio epistolarum D. Pauli* is made by James M. Osborn in *John Dryden: Some Biographical Facts and Problems*, rev. ed. (Gainesville, 1965), p. 245; Osborn, however, does not give serious consideration to the possibility that Dryden may have found use for such a commentary. From the rather limited evidence that there is no reference to such a commentary in Dryden's works, Osborn concludes that the medieval manuscript probably belonged to another John Dryden. There is also a possibility that Dryden made rather extensive book purchases in the areas of theology, liturgy, church government, and church history in May of 1682; see T. A. Birrell, "John Dryden's Purchases at Two Book Auctions, 1680 and 1682," *English Studies* 42 (1961):193–217. Birrell's article is reviewed negatively by James M. Osborn in *Philological Quarterly* 41 (1962):580; but Sanford Budick, in his recent book *Dryden and the Abyss of Light: A Study of "Religio Laici" and "The Hind and the Panther"* (New Haven, 1970),

p. 246, n. 3, supports Birrell's contention that the purchaser was John Dryden the poet.

30. On the Trinity College, Cambridge, Vulgate with *Glossa Ordinaria* and commentary by Nicholas de Lira, see Miner, *Dryden's Poetry*, p. 152.

31. *The Sermons of John Donne,* ed. Evelyn M. Simpson and George R. Potter, 10 vols. (Berkeley and Los Angeles, 1953–62), 2:69.

32. Lancelot Andrewes, *Sermons,* ed. G. M. Story (Oxford, 1967), pp. 200–201.

33. Rosemond Tuve, for example, in *A Reading of George Herbert* (Chicago, 1952), has made extensive and significant use of medieval devotional art in explicating Herbert; images in Donne and Crashaw have been unfolded through the use of patristic and medieval scriptural commentary.

34. James Preus, *From Shadow to Promise: Old Testament Interpretation from Augustine to the Young Luther* (Cambridge, Mass., 1969), p. 20.

35. *Sermons of John Donne,* 4:60.

36. See Preus, *From Shadow to Promise,* pp. 196–97.

37. Bercovitch, *Horologicals to Chronometricals,* p. 8.

38. Ibid.

39. William Lamont, *Godly Rule: Politics and Religion, 1603–1660* (London, 1969), p. 23; Lamont is reaffirming William Haller's thesis about Foxe in Haller's *Elect Nation* (New York, 1963). See also Leonard J. Trinterud, "The Origins of Puritanism," *Church History* 20 (1951):37–57.

40. Preus, *From Shadow to Promise,* p. 197. The general sense of Preus's argument concerning the shift in Luther's interpretation of the Psalms seems to me very convincing, though Preus's exact location of that shift in specific readings has been questioned; see John J. Pilch, "Luther's Hermeneutical 'Shift,' " *Harvard Theological Review* 63 (1970):445–48. Ernest Lee Tuveson's analysis of the reversal of the Augustinian interpretation of history in Reformation thought is relevant to Preus's reading of medieval and Reformation exegetical theory; see Tuveson, *Redeemer Nation: The Idea of America's Millennial Role* (Chicago, 1968), preface, chap. 1. John F. Wilson in his recent book, *Pulpit in Parliament* (Princeton, 1969), explores the notion of "covenanted salvation" with reference to the Puritan sermon literature of the civil war period, confirming Haller and others who trace the scriptural interpretation of English history back to the general impact that Reformed theology had on English religious and political thought, and specifically to Foxe's *Book of Martyrs.*

41. The analogy between Elizabeth and David comes from William Leigh's sermon *Queene Elizabeth, Paraleld in her Princely vertues* (London, 1612), which I discuss at length in chapter 2. The English were not, of course, the only people to offer scriptural interpretations of political events and public figures; we can find similar scriptural readings of contemporary affairs in sixteenth- and seventeenth-century France, Germany, and Netherlands. See, e. g., Jean Métezeau's lengthy portrait of Henri IV as David at the beginning of Métezeau's translation

of *CL Psaumes de David* (1611); or the political allegory in Caron's *Abraham et Melchisédech,* discussed by Roger Trinquet in "L'Allégorie Politique dans la Peinture Française au Temps de la Ligue: L'*Abraham et Melchisédech* d'Antoine Caron," *Bibliothèque d'Humanisme et Renaissance* 28 (1966):636–67; or the politically informed scriptural allusions in the Valois Tapestries, analyzed by Frances A. Yates in *The Valois Tapestries* (London, 1959), pp. 25, 34, 37, 97.

42. *The Works of Robert Harris . . . now collected into one volume* (London, 1635), sig. N6.

43. *Two Sermons . . . upon occasion of Her Majesties happy conception . . . upon the Birth of the Prince* (London, 1688), sig. A2.

44. See, e. g., the verse in *Moestissimae . . . Academiae Cantabrigiensis affectus* (Cambridge, 1684/5), sigs. Bb3–Bb3v, or the Charles-Solomon comparison in Sir F[rancis] F[ane], *A Pindarick Ode on the Sacred Memory of our late Gracious Sovereign King Charles II* (London, 1685).

45. London, 1662.

46. Ernst Kantorowicz, *The King's Two Bodies* (Princeton, 1957), pp. 88, 47.

47. *The Holy State and the Profane State,* ed. Maximilian G. Walten, 2 vols. (New York, 1938), 2:349.

48. *Threnodia Augustalis,* l. 258.

49. In Dante's reading of Psalm 114, for example, *allegory* is used to designate the christological meaning of Moses leading the Israelites out of Egypt: "If we consider the *letter* alone, the departure of the children of Israel from Egypt in the time of Moses is signified; if the *allegory,* our redemption accomplished by Christ is signified; if the *moral meaning,* the conversion of the soul from the sorrow and misery of sin to a state of grace is signified; if the *anagogical,* the departure of the sanctified soul from the slavery of this corruption to the liberty of everlasting glory" ("Letter to the Can Grande della Scala," in *A Translation of Dante's Eleven Letters,* trans. C. S. Latham [London, 1918], p. 193).

50. *The Works* (London, 1631), chap. 4.

51. Walter W. Skeat, *An Etymological Dictionary of the English Language* (Oxford, 1910), p. 14.

52. The definition of *allegory* that I offer here is a functional one devised for the purpose of distinguishing allegory from typology. For a fuller discussion of the idea of allegory in literary forms, see Edward A. Bloom, "The Allegorical Principle," *ELH* 18 (1951):163–90. Michael Murrin's recent book, *The Veil of Allegory* (Chicago, 1969), offers an interesting rhetorical approach to the problem of allegory in Renaissance critical and imaginative literature.

53. *The Poetical Works of Edmund Spenser,* ed. J. C. Smith and E. De Selincourt (London, 1912), p. 407.

54. *Defense of Poesy,* in *Elizabethan Critical Essays,* ed. G. Gregory Smith, 2 vols. (Oxford, 1904), 1:167.

55. *English Literary Criticism: The Renaissance,* ed. O. B. Hardison, Jr. (New York, 1963), p. 46.

56. Ibid., pp. 177–78.

57. "An Account of the Greatest English Poets," in *The Annual Miscellany: For the Year 1694* (London, 1694), p. 319.

58. Auerbach, *Scenes*, p. 54.

59. Alan Roper, *Dryden's Poetic Kingdoms* (London, 1965).

60. Ibid., p. 19.

61. To point out that Roper does not respond to these matters is, however, simply to say that he chose to write one sort of book and not another. My basic argument is that *analogy,* as a total description of Dryden's use of sacred history, fails to make particular the kinds of meaning that the seventeenth century assigned to the Old Testament—meanings that seventeenth-century poets and divines found repeated use for in devotional as well as political contexts and that are important both to the design of Dryden's political poems and to his conception of English history.

62. *Upon the Death of the Lord Hastings,* l. 38. All Dryden quotations are from *The Poems of John Dryden,* ed. James Kinsley, 4 vols. (Oxford, 1958).

CHAPTER 2

1. In his informative doctoral dissertation, "Sighs from Sion: A Study of Radical Puritan Eschatology in England, 1640–1660," (Columbia University, 1966), Frederick S. Plotkin gives the impression that the application of Old Testament history to seventeenth-century England is a characteristic mainly of radical Puritan thought. Yet the material from which he quotes in discussing exegetical method and in illustrating such motifs as Sion or Davidic kingship is by no means exclusively radical Puritan literature. The selections from sermons and political poetry that are cited in this chapter will, I believe, demonstrate that political typology was used by Puritan and Anglican alike, both by supporters of Parliament and of the king. On the general significance of Scripture and theology to Reformation political thought, see George H. Sabine's introduction to *The Works of Gerrard Winstanley,* ed. Sabine (Ithaca, 1941); and Sabine's *History of Political Theory* (New York, 1937), p. 354: "The Protestant Reformation mixed political theory with differences of religious belief and with questions of theological dogma more closely than had been the case even in the Middle Ages. There is, however, no simple formula for this relationship. Everywhere political theories were defended with theological arguments and political alliances were made in the name of religious truth." See also J. H. M. Salmon's *French Religious Wars in English Political Thought* (Oxford, 1959), esp. pp. 28–38.

2. Although it is clear that after the Restoration Dryden's political sentiments were firmly Royalist and monarchist, the importance of the Puritan background to Dryden's thought should not be underestimated. Perhaps it is setting up too firm a dichotomy to say that by linking Christian and classical heroism Dryden was disavowing the Puritan

tradition, as does Arthur W. Hoffman in *John Dryden's Imagery* (Gainesville, 1962), p. 18. Dryden was raised in a family with strong ties to dissenting divines and politics. His grandfather had been a patron of the Puritan divine John Dod, and both paternal and maternal families sided with Parliament in the civil war. Sir Erasmus Dryden had been imprisoned by Charles I for refusing to lend money to the crown; Dryden's father was supposed to have been a committeeman under the Commonwealth; and the poet's first cousin Sir Gilbert Pickering was a judge at the king's trial and later chamberlain to Cromwell. Moreover, the choice of Cambridge for Dryden instead of the traditional family school, Oxford, is an indication of the Puritan leanings of Dryden's immediate family. See Charles Ward, *The Life of John Dryden* (Chapel Hill, 1961), for a fuller discussion of Dryden's Puritan background; see also the *Dictionary of National Biography*, s.v. "Dryden, John."

3. *The Poetry of Limitation: A Study of Edmund Waller* (New Haven, 1968) by Warren Chernaik and the excellent study of Marvell's political poetry by John M. Wallace, *Destiny His Choice: The Loyalism of Andrew Marvell* (Cambridge, 1968), are both indications of a major reassessment of political poetry in mid-seventeenth-century England. So also are the recent Oxford editions of the poetry of King and Cleveland and the Yale edition of *Poems on Affairs of State*. The study of seventeenth-century public poetry by Ruth Nevo, *The Dial of Virtue* (Princeton, 1963), provides a useful survey of the terrain, and C. V. Wedgewood's *Poetry and Politics under the Stuarts* (Cambridge, 1960) sketches the political context but does not attempt rigorous literary analysis.

4. I refer to the estimates of Dryden in Harold Fisch's *Jerusalem and Albion* (New York, 1964), pp. 259 ff.; and Murray Roston's *Prophet and Poet* (Evanston, 1965), pp. 288–97; as well as to the more recent publications of A. L. French, "Dryden, Marvell and Political Poetry," *Studies in English Literature* 8 (1968):397–413; Anne D. Ferry, *Milton and the Miltonic Dryden* (Cambridge, Mass., 1968); and Leon M. Guilhamet, "Dryden's Debasement of Scripture in *Absalom and Achitophel*," *Studies in English Literature* 9 (1969):395–413.

5. See R. F. Jones, "The Originality of *Absalom and Achitophel*," *Modern Language Notes* 46 (1931):211–18.

6. Frances A. Yates, in her study "Queen Elizabeth as Astraea," *Journal of the Warburg and Courtauld Institutes* 10 (1947):27–82, offers a wealth of literary and pictorial materials to support her discussion of classical iconography in representations of the queen.

7. See William Haller, *The Elect Nation* (New York, 1963), and Charles H. and Katherine George, *The Protestant Mind of the English Reformation* (Princeton, 1961), both of which serve as a good introduction to the growth of English Puritanism and treat the way in which the English as a Protestant nation developed a providential and scriptural interpretation of their fate. William A. Clebsch, in *England's Earliest Protestants* (New Haven, 1964), provides a discussion of the impact of continental Reformation theology on English Protestant thought.

8. The Puritan divine and nonconformist leader Joseph Caryl, in *Davids Prayer for Solomon* (London, 1643), sig. D2, offers a representative statement of the covenant mentality, an important aspect of Puritan thought: "It is a truth indeed, that the people of *Israel* were Gods people, in a more peculiar manner, then any whole Nation upon the earth is at this time; there is no whole Nation hath such a priviledge, and are the people of God in so strict a sence, as they were, for they were all as a Church, and Christ had as many subjects among the *Jews,* as the King had; because they were all at once taken into covenant with God; It is not so in any Nation now upon the earth. But yet God hath his speciall Covenant people, his peculiar ones in every Nation, who are the speciall charge of Princes; and though all others are Gods people, as men, and the Princes charge too, yet for the sake of these chiefely, Governours are set up, and Princes sit upon the Throne." Boyd Berry, in "The Doctrine of the Remnant 1550–1660: A Study in the History of English Puritanism and *Paradise Lost*" (Ph.D. diss., University of Michigan, 1966), offers an interesting discussion of the relationship between remnant political thought and typological exegesis. The history of covenant political thought has been charted most fully with respect to English Puritans in America. See Perry Miller, *The New England Mind: Colony to Province* (Cambridge, Mass., 1953); Kenneth B. Murdock, "Clio in the Wilderness: History and Biography in Puritan New England," *Church History* 24 (1955):221–38; and essays by Sacvan Bercovitch: "New England Epic: Cotton Mather's *Magnalia Christi Americana,*" ELH 33 (1966):337–51; "Typology in Puritan New England: The Williams-Cotton Controversy Reassessed," *American Quarterly* 19 (1967):166–91; and "The Historiography of Johnson's *Wonder-Working Providence,*" *Essex Institute Historical Collections* 104 (1968):138–61.

9. Elizabeth's popularity as the patron monarch of the Protestant cause is attested to well into the Restoration period by the annual Pope-burning procession held on 17 November, the anniversary of Elizabeth's accession. See *Poems on Affairs of State* (New Haven, 1963–), vol. 2, ed. Elias Mengel, Jr. (1965), p. xxviii.

10. London, 1612. Leigh, an Oxford graduate, was chaplain to Henry, earl of Derby, and later tutor to James I's eldest son, Prince Henry. Leigh was a preacher at court, an active man in public life, and "was held in great esteem for his learning and godliness." See the *Dictionary of National Biography,* s.v. "Leigh, William."

11. Sigs. B2–B2v. The ark as a type of God's Church is one of the most common biblical types. Augustine used it in his exegesis *De civitate Dei* 15. 26. Cf. John Weemse's seventeenth-century interpretation in *An Explanation of the ceremoniall Lawes of Moses, as they are annexed to the teene commandements* (London, 1632), sig. C3: "The fluctuant Arke of *Noah* signified the tossed and troubled estate of the Church in the world here, it is represented also by the ship in which Christ and his Apostles were; this ship was mightily tossed, and Christ was sleeping in the meanetime in the ship, the Disciples cryed out and bad Christ awake, for they were ready to perish, and Christ awoke and calmed the

storme; the fluctuant Arke is like the Church tossed to and fro, and Christ in the mean time seemeth to be sleeping, yet he hath a care that the barke perish not." Francis Roberts, in *Mysterium and Medulla Bibliorum* (London, 1657), sig. Mm1, summarized the typological interpretation of the story of Noah in a brief fashion: "*Noah*, was a singular Type of Christ; The Ark, a figure of the Church; and the temporal saving of his House with himself in the Ark by water, a special type of the salvation of Christs Elect in the Church by Jesus Christ." Other expositions can be found in the typology manuals considered in chap. 1: William Guild, *Moses unveiled* (London, 1658); Samuel Mather, *The Figures or Types* (Dublin, 1683); and Thomas Taylor, *Moses and Aaron; or, the Types and Shadows of our Saviour in the old Testament* (London, 1653).

12. Sigs. D7–D8v.

13. Sig. E3.

14. The inclusion of the present moment in the dynamics of a typological relationship is important to an understanding both of devotional typology, with its stress on the state of the individual soul, and of political typology, with its emphasis on the condition of the corporate elect. Thus, in federal theology, the " 'atonement accomplished in Jesus Christ ceases to be the history of the Covenant, to which (in all the different forms of expectation and recollection) the whole Bible bears witness . . . and it becomes a (stage in) biblical history, a stage in the greater context of world history, before which and after which there are other similar stages' " (Karl Barth, *Church Dogmatics* [Edinburgh, 1956], 4:56, quoted in J. L. Scott, "The Covenant in the Theology of Karl Barth," *Scottish Journal of Theology* 17 [1964]:185–86).

15. Sigs. E5v–E6.

16. Sig. E6. See the discussion above, pp. 10–11, of Brinsley's *Mystical Brasen Serpent* for a seventeenth-century distinction between analogy (similitude) and typology. Cf. Richard Bernard's *Seaven Golden Candlestickes* (London, 1621), sig. F1v: "Hee that receiveth much, oweth much, and is bound to love the more. Let mee say as once *Moses* did, the name *Israel* being changed into *England*. *And now* (O England) *what doth the Lord thy God require*. . . . That so (as God himselfe wished to Israel) it might go well with us and with our Children for ever."

17. *The Sermons of John Donne*, ed. Evelyn M. Simpson and George R. Potter, 10 vols. (Berkeley and Los Angeles, 1953–62), 2:55.

18. J[ohn] L[ane], *An Elegie upon the death of the high and renowned Princesse, our late Soveraigne Elizabeth* (London, 1603), in *Fugitive Tracts Written in Verse Which Illustrate the Condition of Religious and Political Feeling in England and the State of Society there during Two Centuries*, ed. Henry Huth, 2d ser. (London, 1875), p. [18].

19. Ibid., p. [20].

20. *Sermons of John Donne*, 6:280–91. Dora and Erwin Panofsky, in *Pandora's Box: The Changing Aspects of a Mythical Symbol*, 2d ed.

rev. (New York, 1965), p. 69, note that the identification of the king with Solomon was common. Milton was not quite so impressed with James I. Of the analogies between James and Solomon he wrote: "There were, I admit, some who did not hesitate to compare James, his father, with Solomon, and indeed to prefer the former's descent. Solomon was the son of David, who was originally Saul's musician: James was the son of the Earl of Darnley, who is said by Buchanan to have caught David the musician on a nocturnal visit to his queen's bedroom when he had slipped the bolt, and killed David on the spot" (*A Defence of the People of England* [1651], in *Complete Prose Works of John Milton,* ed. Don M. Wolfe [New Haven, 1953–], vol. 4, ed. Wolfe [1966], pp. 371–72).

21. *Sermons of John Donne,* 6:280–81.

22. Ibid., 6:286.

23. *The Poetical Works of Robert Herrick,* ed. L. C. Martin (Oxford, 1956), p. 86, ll. 19–44.

24. See, e.g., the poem *Caroli* in *Monumentum Regale: or A Tombe, Erected for that incomparable and Glorious Monarch, Charles the First . . . In select elegies, epitaphs, and poems* (n.p., 1649), sigs. B7v–B8:

> He was the only *Moses* that could stand
> Betwixt the *sinnes* and *judgements* of the Land.
> And what can we expect, our *Lot* being gone,
> But that a *Hell* for *Heav'n* should tumble down
> On our more sinful *Sodom?*

25. Milton's application of scriptural example to contemporary political questions can be found both in *The Tenure of Kings and Magistrates* and in *A Defence of the People of England.*

26. *Complete Prose Works,* 4:405–6.

27. See ibid., vol. 3, ed. Merritt Y. Hughes (1962), p. 203, n. 56.

28. Ibid., 3:236.

29. Ibid., vol. 2, ed. Ernest Sirluck (1959), p. 552.

30. See Plotkin's discussion of Puritan sermons in "Sighs from Sion," pp. 68–71, 127–66. John F. Wilson's recent study, *Pulpit in Parliament: Puritanism during the English Civil Wars, 1640–1648* (Princeton, 1969), covers much of the same material; see esp. chap. 6. Wilson's app. 2 provides a list of short titles of sermons preached before members of the Long Parliament when assembled for humiliations and thanksgivings.

31. *Historie and Policie Re-viewed, In The Heroick Transactions of his Most Serene Highnesse, Oliver, Late Lord Protector; From his Cradle, to his Tomb: Declaring his steps to Princely Perfection; as they are drawn in lively Parallels to the Ascents of the Great Patriarch Moses, in thirty Degrees, to the Height of Honour* (London, 1659), sig. E5v.

32. *Satan the Leader in chief to all who resist the Reparation of Sion* (London, 1643), sigs. B2v, G3v.

33. For a general treatment of the political activities of the radical Puritans, see P. G. Rogers, *The Fifth Monarchy Men* (London, 1966).

34. (Oxford, 1643), sigs. A2v–A6.

35. Plotkin, "Sighs from Sion," chap. 4.

36. Plotkin, in "Sighs from Sion," confirms this view: "In an important sense, then, the figure of David after 1660 is the figure of royalty—whether of the secular, ecclesiastical, or Divine realms— emerged from its eclipse and restored to its proper place" (p. 121). Plotkin, however, has a tendency to see the post-Restoration uses of providential history as a direct product of Puritan interregnum thought. He writes, for example: "Using the Puritan sense of England's sacred history, Charles was seen by some post-Restoration exegetes as the chief of God's providentially Elect" (p. 120). However, as has been shown earlier in this chapter, the concept of an elect England was not the exclusive property of radical Puritan thought but widespread during the whole century.

37. *God and the King: or, a Dialogue, shewing, That our Soveraign Lord . . . doth rightly claim whatsoever is required by the Oath of Allegiance* (London, 1663), sig. C4v. The first edition of *God and the King* (London, 1615) was compiled and printed "by the especial Command of King James"; the 1663 edition has an engraving of Charles II, with a crown held above his head by two angels, and the inscription "By Mee Kings Raine." See also T[homas] B[ayly], *The Royal Charter granted unto Kings by God himself: and collected out of his Holy Word, in both Testaments* (London, 1649), chaps. 3, 4.

38. See Francis Oakley, "Jacobean Political Theology: the Absolute and Ordinary Powers of the King," *Journal of the History of Ideas* 29 (1968):323–46. On the significance of royal consecration in Renaissance France, see R. J. Knecht, *Francis I and Absolute Monarchy* (London, 1969), p. 5. Isaac Penington, in *Expositions with observations,* (London, 1656), deals with the significance of anointment in his chapter "The Anointing and Function of Christ."

39. The coronation ceremony was recorded by John Ogilby in *The Entertainment of . . . Charles II, in his passage through the city of London to his coronation . . . To these is added a . . . narrative of his Majestie's . . . Coronation* (London, 1662), sig. Bb3v.

40. *The Poems of John Cleveland,* ed. Brian Morris and Eleanor Withington (Oxford, 1967), pp. 8–9, ll. 91–98.

41. Morris and Withington, in their commentary on the poem, remark about this analogy that "Solomon, one of the 'dusky types' or prefigurations of Christ, is seen here as a prefiguration of King Charles as well" (ibid., p. 91). But there seems to be no more reason for Solomon to prefigure Charles than for Solomon and Charles to participate in the more conventional foreshadowing and reflecting of Christ.

42. Ibid., p. 9, ll. 115–24. Ruth Nevo, in *The Dial of Virtue,* discusses the poem as a "good example of Cleveland's panegyric method" (pp. 45–46). However, her discussion is marred by a curious misreading; she takes the phrase "mouldy bread, and clouted shooes" to be a metaphorical description of the king's disguise rather than of the Scots, with whom the king makes a league in giving up his person to them. The scriptural passage to which the phrase alludes (Josh. 9) confirms my reading.

43. *Poems of John Cleveland,* p. lxvi.

44. The execution-crucifixion literature on Charles I flourished in verse, sermon, and pamphlet forms. Helen W. Randall's article "The Rise and Fall of a Martyrology: Sermons on Charles I," *Huntington Library Quarterly* 10 (1946):135–67, provides an introductory survey of the sermon literature. Arthur E. Case's *Bibliography of English Poetical Miscellanies, 1521–1750* (Oxford, 1935) cites the relevant verse collections. Joseph Frank's *Hobbled Pegasus* (Albuquerque, 1968) provides an informative and amusing bibliographical survey of the minor verse, from broadside and short pamphlets to full books, published in English between 1641 and 1660. The *Catalogue of the Pamphlets . . . Collected by G. Thomason*, ed. G. K. Fortescue, 2 vols. (London, 1908), is the basic bibliographical guide to the relevant pamphlet materials.

45. *The Monument of Charles the first, King of England* [London, 1649]; the verse is arranged in two columns beneath an engraving of the tomb.

46. *Caroli*, sig. B6v.

47. This topic is discussed in Emile Mâle's *The Gothic Image* (New York, 1958), in the chapter entitled "Secular History," and in several places by Otto von Simson in *The Gothic Cathedral* (New York, 1956). See esp. von Simson's remarks on the Capetian dynasty and Charlemagne, pp. 137–38; 140–41; 180–81.

48. *The Devilish Conspiracy, Hellish Treason, Heathenish Condemnation, and Damnable Murder, committed, and executed by the Jewes, against . . . Christ their King . . . As it was delivered in a sermon on the 4 Feb. 1648* (London, 1648). Warner was the Bishop of Rochester, a "devoted adherent of the Church and Monarchy," and chaplain to Charles I; see the *Dictionary of National Biography*, s.v. "Warner, John." Another example of this play on the king and Christ comes from the *Autobiography of Thomas Raymond*, ed. G. Davies (London, 1917), pp. 59–60. Raymond records the following scene: "Soone after our most gratious King Charles the First was by hellish miscreants sonnes of Belial put to death, it was my chance to be in London at sermon in St. Mary Alder-Maryes Church, it being death then for any man and especially ministers to speake in vindication of that good King. The preacher fell to aggravate the great synnes whereof wee were guilty and haveing instanced in severall greate and crying ones, 'Nay,' said he, 'wee have put to death our King, our most gracious and good King'—at which he made a little pause (the people amazed and gazing aboute expecting the preacher should be pulled out of the pulpitt) but he added—'the Lord Jesus Christ by our sinnes and transgression.' "

49. See, e.g., J. W.'s *King Charles I. his imitation of Christ. Or the parallel lines of our Saviours and our kings sufferings; drawn through fourty six texts of Scripture. In an English and French Poem* (London, 1660); or *On the Martyrdom of King Charles the First, January the 30th: 1648. A Pindaric Ode*, in "Miscellaneous Poems and Tracts, 1681–1703," 2 vols., William Andrews Clark Memorial Library, Los Angeles. Sermon literature on the execution abounds in such parallels; see, e.g.,

Henry Leslie's sermon *The Martyrdome of King Charles, or his conformity with Christ in his sufferings* (the Hague, 1649); and T[homas] L[ambert]'s *Sad Memorials of the Royal Martyr: or, a Parallel betwixt the Jewes murder of Christ, and the English murder of King Charls the First: being a sermon preached on the solemnity of His Majesties martyrdom* (London, 1670).

50. *A Deepe Groane, fetch'd at the Funerall of that incomparable and Glorious Monarch, Charles the First, King of Great Britaine, France, and Ireland, &c.,* in *The Poems of Henry King,* ed. M. Crum (Oxford, 1965), p. 113.

51. *An Elegie Upon King Charles the First, murthered publikely by His Subjects,* sig. C5v.

52. Joseph Mazzeo, "Cromwell as Davidic King," in *Reason and the Imagination,* ed. Mazzeo (New York, 1962), pp. 29–55.

53. Ibid., p. 45. Of the passage beginning with l. 105, which presents a reading of Cromwell's government in apocalyptic terms, Mazzeo writes, "It is a little odd to follow Marvell through a prophetic interpretation of Cromwell in the apocalyptic mode (105–58) where his rule is seen as a preparation for the fulfillment of biblical prophecy." Perhaps it is a little odd if one approaches the passage only from the point of view of medieval typology; but, as we have seen, the Puritans commonly applied biblical prophecy to contemporary political events.

54. *The Poems and Letters of Andrew Marvell,* ed. H. M. Margoliouth, 2d ed., 2 vols. (Oxford, 1952), 1:109, ll. 249–56.

55. John Diodati, *Pious and Learned Annotations upon the Holy Bible* (London, 1648), sig. K8.

56. See commentary in *The Works of John Dryden,* ed. E. N. Hooker and H. T. Swedenberg, Jr. (Berkeley and Los Angeles, 1956–), vol. 1, ed. Hooker and Swedenberg, p. 212.

57. This is the opinion of French, Ferry, and Guilhamet; see n. 4 to this chapter.

58. London, 1661. A strong, though not active, Royalist, Boteler was made one of Charles II's chaplains after the Restoration; see the *Dictionary of National Biography,* s.v. "Boteler, Edward."

59. Sigs. B1–B1v.

60. Augustine, *De civitate Dei* 13. 21.

61. Erich Auerbach, *Mimesis* (New York, 1957), p. 64.

62. Sigs. B6v, B7.

63. See, e.g., Giles Fleming's pamphlet *Stemma Sacrum; the royal progeny delineated, and with some notes explained, shewing his Sacred Majesties royal and lawful descent . . . from all the kings that ever reigned in this nation* (London, 1660). On the title page Fleming cites Ecclesiastes 10:17 and 2 Kings 19:30. The former stresses the divinity and noble descent of the king; the latter invokes the remnant motif, a favorite theme in Puritan literature. The dedicatory essay expands on both themes.

64. *A Sermon preached . . . before the . . . House of Commons . . . upon the anniversary day of the King's and Kingdomes restauration* (London, 1661), sigs. D1v–D2.

65. Ibid., sigs. E3–E3v.

66. See also the various satires employing biblical schemes in *Poems on Affairs of State;* e.g., John Caryll's *Naboth's Vineyard,* in vol. 2, ed. Elias Mengel, Jr. (1965), p. 83.

67. (London, 1660), sig. C1.

68. Oxford, 1660.

69. *A sermon preached at White-Hall on the 29th . . . May 1661; being the . . . day of his Majesties inauguration and birth* (London, 1661), sigs. A3v–A4.

70. Quoted from Narcissus Luttrell's collection of tracts, ballads, and broadsides "Poetry longwaies, 1683–1685," item 43, sig. E1, William Andrews Clark Memorial Library, Los Angeles.

71. See, e.g., John Guy's *On the happy accession of their Majesties King William and Queen Mary . . . A Pindarique ode* (London, 1699), sig. E1. In Edward Nicholas's *Ode,* in the collection *Vota Oxoniensa* (Oxford, 1689), William is a "second Moses, whose avenging Rod / Wav'd o're the Land does set it free / At once from Pharaohs Gods and Pharaohs slavery" (sig. 2Z).

72. *Britannia Rediviva: or, Britain's recovery* (London, 1714), p. 9.

73. See Victor Harris, "Allegory to Analogy in the Interpretation of Scriptures," *Philological Quarterly* 45 (1966):1–23.

74. (London), p. vi. Annet's authorship of the volume is in some doubt; the *History* has also been attributed to Archibald Campbell, M. Huet, and John Noorthouck. On the question of authorship, see *Notes and Queries,* 1st ser., 12 (1855):214; and Halkett and Laing's *Dictionary of Anonymous and Pseudonymous English Literature* (Edinburgh, 1928), 3:86.

CHAPTER 3

1. Johnson, *Lives of the Poets,* ed. G. B. Hill, 3 vols. (Oxford, 1905), 1:399; Scott, ed., *The Works of John Dryden,* 15 vols., rev. G. Saintsbury (Edinburgh, 1882–93), 9:30; Hooper, ed., *Dryden's Poetical Works,* 5 vols. (London, 1891), 1:xiv; Van Doren, *John Dryden: A Study of his Poetry,* 3d ed. (New York, 1946), p. 111; Kinsley, "Dryden and the Art of Praise," *English Studies* 34 (1953):59; Miner, *Dryden's Poetry* (Bloomington, Ind., 1967), p. 6.

2. See, e.g., Rosemond Tuve, *A Reading of George Herbert* (Chicago, 1952); Dennis Quinn, "John Donne's Principles of Biblical Exegesis," *Journal of English and Germanic Philology* 61 (1962):313–29; and Frank Manley, ed., *John Donne: "The Anniversaries"* (Baltimore, 1963). Milton's use of typology is discussed in Barbara K. Lewalski's *Milton's Brief Epic* (Providence, 1966) and William G. Madsen's *From Shadowy Types to Truth* (New Haven, 1968).

3. Although I disagree with some of Joseph Mazzeo's specific readings (as discussed in chap. 2 above), his essay "Cromwell as Davidic King," in *Reason and the Imagination,* ed. Mazzeo (New York, 1962), is an

important exception to the past neglect of biblical typology in seventeenth-century political verse. And both the recent essay by Paul J. Korshin, "The Evolution of Neoclassical Poetics: Cleveland, Denham, and Waller as Poetic Theorists," *Eighteenth-Century Studies* 2 (1968):102–38, and the article by George Levine, "Dryden's 'Inarticulate Poesy': Music and the Davidic King in *Absalom and Achitophel*," *Eighteenth-Century Studies* 1 (1968):291–312, indicate that studies in later seventeenth-century literature are moving toward an appreciation of the place of sacred history and biblical typology in political poetry.

4. *The Works of John Dryden*, ed. E. N. Hooker and H. T. Swedenberg, Jr. (Berkeley and Los Angeles, 1956–), vol. 1, ed. Hooker and Swedenberg, p. 208; H. J. Oliver, *Sir Robert Howard: A Critical Biography* (Durham, N.C., 1963), p. 15. Oliver writes: "Already Dryden was showing his Jonsonian art of adapting the tribute to the receiver; even if the compliment was not deserved, it was, on the whole, neatly paid."

5. Oliver, *Howard*, pp. 28–29. The *Achilleid* 3. 218–20 reads: "At length, his Mother's craft he did disclose, / A grove there was, whose top to Heav'n arose. / Sacred to *Bacchus*." Howard glosses the sacred grove with reference to Virgil in the *Aeneid* 1 and *Georgics* 3; to Suetonius in *Augusto*; to Juvenal in *Satires* 3. 296; and to Joshua 24:26. In referring to Joshua, Howard quotes the commentator Mede, who "sheweth that the Jewes had their praying places, besides their Synagogues, out of a notable place of *Epiphanius*, a Jew bred and born in *Palestine*" (*Poems: viz. 1, A Panegyrick to the king . . . a Panegyrick to General Monck* [London, 1660], sig. R8). Another example of Howard's accommodation of the classical to the scriptural is his gloss on the ceremony of throwing entrails into the waves: "This custom, among others, which in the Notes I have given short hints of, was taken up by the Heathen in imitation of the true God's worship; as will appear from Levit. 1.9, 13. *The inwards and the legs shall he wash in water, and the Priest shall burn all on the Altar.* Of the Priests eating part of the sacrifice, see Levit. 23.10. and 6.26. *Ecclus.* 7.31" (sig. U3v).

6. For a discussion of classical myth in the Nativity ode, see Lewalski, *Milton's Brief Epic*, p. 175. Renaissance commentaries such as Boccacio's *Genealogia Deorum Gentilium* (1547) and Comes's *Mythologiae: Sive Explicationis Fabularum* (1605), and translations of Ovid such as Sandys's *Ovid's Metamorphosis Englished, Mythologiz'd, and Represented in Figures* (1632), are familiar sources of the accommodation of classical myth to biblical and Christian models. The use that Renaissance culture made of classical mythology is treated in Douglas Bush, *Mythology and the Renaissance Tradition in English Poetry*, rev. ed. (New York, 1963); Jean Seznec, *The Survival of the Pagan Gods* (New York, 1953); Edgar Wind, *Pagan Mysteries in the Renaissance*, rev. ed. (London, 1968); and Frances A. Yates, *The French Academies of the Sixteenth Century* (London, 1947), chap. 7.

7. See, e.g., Bacon, *De Sapientia Veterum*, in *Works*, ed. J. Spedding et al., 14 vols. (Cambridge, 1857–74), 13:84–87.

8. Alexander Ross, e.g., read the myth in the following terms: "The

Devil is the very *Typhon,* who by his pride opposed God, and was thrust down to hell: the greatness of *Typhons* body argues the greatness of Satans power; his snaky hands and serpentine feet do shew, that his actions and ways are cunning and deadly" (*Mystagogus Poeticus; or the Muses Interpreter: Explaining The Historical Mysteries and Mystical Histories of the Antient Greek and Latin Poets,* 6th ed. [London, 1675], sig. Dd1v). Davis P. Harding, in *Milton and the Renaissance Ovid* (Urbana, 1946), pp. 85–88, offers further evidence for the association of Typhon with Satan in sixteenth- and seventeenth-century literature.

9. See *Works of John Dryden,* 1:223.

10. "Annotations on Genesis," in *Choice Observations and Explanations Upon the Old Testament* (London, 1655), sigs. B3v–B4. For William Guild, Enoch is "reported and brought in as one that saw not death, but was translated, *Gen.* 5. 24. *To yield that comfort to the Church, and type Christ therein, who should make death to be swallowd up in victory, and immortality, and to assure us also of the resurrection*" (*Moses unveiled* [London, 1658], sig. B5v).

11. *Paradise Lost* 12. 303.

12. *Works of John Dryden,* 1:233.

13. Ibid., 1:219. Eberhard Späth, in *Dryden als Poeta Laureatus* (Nuremberg, 1969), p. 28, makes the following remarks about Hooker and Swedenberg's commentary on Dryden's presentation of Charles II in terms of Davidic and christic analogies: "Die Kommentatoren der neuen amerikanischen Dryden-Ausgabe erklären diese Bilder als Ausdruck überschwenglicher Freude über die Restauration. . . . Abgesehen von der Tatsche, dass Dryden von seinen Biographen als skeptischer Mensch geschildert wird, der nicht zu Gefühlsausbrüchen neigte, wirkt auch seine Bildersprache eher bewusst und überlegt gestaltet als emotional. Wenn Karl II. mit Gott und Christus verglichen oder mit David, dem Vorläufer des Messias, identifiziert wird, so kann dies nicht auf Gefühlsübersteigerung zurückgeführt werden; vielmehr deutet dies auf das Verhältnis hin, das nach Drydens Meinung und nach der zeitgenössischen royalistischen Theorie zwischen Gott und dem König besteht." Späth's monograph, which presents some of the same conclusions as this study of Dryden's political poetry, came to my attention after the present text had been completed.

14. See Bernard Schilling, *Dryden and the Conservative Myth* (New Haven, 1961), p. 270. In his remarks on the similarities between *Astraea Redux* and *Absalom and Achitophel* Schilling points to several interesting relationships; but in stressing the image of Charles as healer and savior in the earlier poem he neglects the transformed image of the king in the concluding passages of *Astraea Redux.*

15. Alan Roper, *Dryden's Poetic Kingdoms* (London, 1965), pp. 73–74.

16. *Moses unveiled,* sig. B7.

17. London, 1653. Of the relationship between Noah and Christ, Taylor writes: "Both of them were repairers of the world. From *Noah* descended all the inhabitants of the earth: from Christ all the inhabitants of heaven. The world again was re-peopled and replenished

by *Noahs* posterity: the Church and every memeber is Christs posterity.
Both of them were preservers and providers for all sorts of Creatures:
But *Noah* as a steward; Christ as Lord and owner of them: *Noah* for a
few, Christ for all: *Noah* for a year and a little more, Christ perpetually.
To both of them the creatures came in, and were obedient to them.
Though never so fierce and savage out of the Ark, yet in the Ark they
were mild and tame: So to Christ the windes, seas, devils obey; and if
Lyons and Cockatrices come into the Ark and Church, they become as
Lambs and little children, putting off all fiercenesse" (sigs. B6–B6v).
For other seventeenth-century readings of Noah see Guild, *Moses
unveiled;* John Weemse, *An Explanation of the ceremonial Lawes of
Moses* (London, 1632); Francis Roberts, *Mysterium & Medulla
Bibliorum* (London, 1657); and Samuel Mather, *The Figures or Types*
(Dublin, 1683).

    18. Augustine, *De civitate Dei* 20. 2. 1–30.

    19. *Works of John Dryden*, 1:236.

    20. (London), bk. 2, sig. Ee. This is not the same work listed in
Donald G. Wing's *Short-title Catalogue of Books . . . 1641–1700* as K85
(*Scripture Metaphors* [London, 1681]) or K101 (Τρυποσχημαλογια: *Tropes
and Figures* [London, 1682]). The work to which I refer does not appear
in Wing but has the British Museum *Catalogue* number 3109. h. 8.

    21. *Moses and Aaron*, sigs. R6–R6v.

    22. As Milton asserts, "The essence of God, being in itself most
simple, can admit no compound quality; so that the term *hypostasis*
Heb. 1.3. which is differently translated *substance,* or *subsistence,* or
person, can be nothing else but the most perfect essence by which God
subsists by himself, in himself, and through himself. For neither
substance nor *subsistence* make any addition to what is already a most
perfect essence" (*Christian Doctrine* 1. 2, in *The Works of John Milton,*
ed. Frank A. Patterson, 18 vols. [New York, 1931–38], vol. 14, ed. James
Holly Hanford and Waldo Hilary Dunn [1933], pp. 41–43).

CHAPTER 4

    1. Jackson I. Cope, in his note "Science, Christ, and Cromwell in
Dryden's *Heroic Stanzas," Modern Language Notes* 71 (1956):483–85,
suggests the possibility of christic references in Dryden's presentation
of Cromwell. As Cope points out, the providential nature of Cromwell's
rule undoubtedly forms part of the subject matter of Dryden's poem;
however, the christic references are, at best, ambiguous. The *"sacred
Eagle"* (l. 4), for example, which Cope cites as an image contributing
to Cromwell's christic meaning, is set in an explicitly Roman, rather
than scriptural, context.

    2. The fullest exposition of the poem's political meaning is Earl R.
Wasserman's "Dryden: *Epistle to Charleton,"* in *The Subtler Language*
(Baltimore, 1959), chap. 2.

    3. This is one of the central ideas in E. N. Hooker, "The Purpose

of Dryden's *Annus Mirabilis,*" *Huntington Library Quarterly* 10
(1946–47):49–67. Earl Miner, in *Dryden's Poetry* (Bloomington, 1967),
pp. 3–35, defends the aesthetic integrity of the poem by arguing for its
consistency of language and design.

4. This is John Diodati's gloss on Moses in Exodus 14:31 (*Pious
Annotations Upon the Holy Bible Expounding the difficult places
thereof Learnedly and Plainly* [London, 1648], sig. D8).

5. Miner, in *Dryden's Poetry,* p. 25, notes the Davidic and christic
associations in the "King's Prayer" but does not fully relate them to the
pattern of scriptural allusion in the poem.

6. *Absalom and Achitophel* has been the subject of extensive
commentary and much appreciation, yet a critical consensus is still to
be reached on Dryden's intent in masking contemporary events in a
biblical tale and the kind of success he achieved in doing so. Miner
(*Dryden's Poetry,* pp. 106–43), Arthur W. Hoffman (*John Dryden's
Imagery* [Gainesville, 1962], pp. 72–92), and Bernard Schilling (*Dryden
and the Conservative Myth* [New Haven, 1961]) have helped to explore
the nature of the metaphor and point to some of the ways in which the
biblical vehicle mediates between the tenors of past and present; yet
there remain a number of unconvinced readers. A. L. French ("Dryden,
Marvell, and Political Poetry," *Studies in English Literature* 8 [1968]:
397–413), Anne D. Ferry (*Milton and the Miltonic Dryden* [Cambridge,
Mass., 1968]), and Leon M. Guilhamet ("Dryden's Debasement of
Scripture in *Absalom and Achitophel,*" *Studies in English Literature*
9 [1969]:395–413) assert that Milton and Marvell were in touch with
the values of an earlier age but that Dryden, servant of brute
Restoration politics, can use biblical and classical parallels only in a
superficial way. The critical attitudes of French, Ferry, and Guilhamet
can be traced to such works of the mid-1960s as Harold Fisch's
*Jerusalem and Albion: The Hebraic Factor in Seventeenth-Century
Literature* (New York, 1964) and Murray Roston's *Prophet and Poet:
The Bible and the Growth of Romanticism* (Evanston, 1965). These
attitudes can, in turn, be found in such works of the 1950s as James
Sutherland's *English Satire* (Cambridge, 1958). And, of course, the
same attitudes find ample expression in nineteenth-century criticism of
Dryden.

7. R. F. Jones, in "The Originality of *Absalom and Achitophel,*"
Modern Language Notes 46 (1931):211–18, was one of the first to
explore the varied use of the Absalom narrative in seventeenth-century
sermon and occasional literature. (For a discussion of seventeenth-
century political applications of sacred history, see chap. 2 of this book.)
William Guild observed of the relationship between Absalom and
Antichrist: "But hereafter did *Absolon* craftily under a faire pretence
of the good of *Israel* rise against *David* and stole away the hearts of
Davids people, who joyned themselves with him in rebellion, many
following him in the simplicity of their hearts, and being deceived by
his simulat and faire pretence of piety: even so did Antichrist arise
against Christ under a like faire pretence to be for him, and therefore
is said to be horned like the lamb, though speaking like the dragon, and

who fraudulently stole away the hearts of Gods people. . . . But as
Absolon was at last overthrown, and *Davids* kingdome under him was
thereafter peaceably established: so shall Antichrist according to that
prediction *Revel.* 18. And the Church of Christ shall thereafter injoy
peace and quietness" (*The Throne of David* [Oxford, 1659], sigs.
A2–A2v).

8. For the exegete Thomas Taylor, David was a type of Christ "first
in respect of his followers, secondly of his enemies, thirdly of his
victories." Taylor is especially interesting when he treats of David's and
Christ's enemies. Among them are Doeg and Achitophel, but Absalom
is singled out for special treatment: "Our true *David* had not onely
his own Jewes and brethren hating him with an horrible hatred, and
calling his bloud upon themselves; but his own Disciple that had been
so familiar with him, that went to the house of God often with him,
that knew all his haunts and waies, betraying him, and delivering him
to be crucified. And thus Christ himselfe expounds that in *Psal.* 41. 9.
of himselfe and *Judas, Luk.* 22. 21. And therefore Interpretors expound
such execrations, as *Psal.* 59. 13. *Consume them that they be no more,*
not so much litterally against *Saul* and other enemies of *David;* as
against the Jewes and enemies of Christ shadowed by them" (*Moses
and Aaron* [London, 1653], sigs. E5–E5v). Thus not only is David a type
of Christ, but the whole history of David among his people is involved
in the figural interpretation of sacred history. I am not insisting that
Dryden was committed to the figural aspect of the story but, rather, that
the narrative from 2 Samuel—especially the relationships between the
main characters—had traditionally admitted of figural interpretation
and that this interpretation was readily available to the seventeenth-
century reader.

9. Barbara K. Lewalski, "The Scope and Function of Biblical
Allusion in *Absalom and Achitophel,*" *English Language Notes* 3
(1965):33.

10. See James Kinsley's gloss on Corah in *The Poems of John Dryden,*
4 vols. (Oxford, 1958), 4:1893–94.

11. Earl Miner's essay "Some Characteristics of Dryden's Use of
Metaphor," *Studies in English Literature* 2 (1962):309–20, offers a
sensitive reading of the ironies and tensions in the opening lines of the
poem. Miner has incorporated those observations into the chapter on
Absalom and Achitophel in his *Dryden's Poetry.* George R. Levine has
adopted Miner's reading in "Dryden's 'Inarticulate Poesy': Music and
the Davidic King in *Absalom and Achitophel,*" *Eighteenth-Century
Studies* 1 (1968):291–312. Levine is concerned with Dryden's handling
of the Davidic *figura,* but in his interpretation of its seventeenth-century
meaning he depends too heavily on definitions from medieval texts,
especially Dante.

12. Thus William Frost holds that Dryden develops the character of
David from a "symbol of weakness (or power dissipated by frivolity),
to a symbol of stability and disinterested justice. . . . our attitude toward
the King, who is at first merely an *idol* (or idle) *monarch, grown in
Bathsheba's embraces old,* shifts, as the whole situation is unrolled

before our eyes, from almost contempt to a feeling that David is the only stable prop against sheer chaos—political, economic, and moral" (*Selected Works of John Dryden,* ed. Frost, 2d ed. [New York, 1971], p. 12). But the line that Frost quotes to characterize David at the opening of the poem ("grown in *Bathsheba*'s Embraces old," l. 710) hardly represents the narrator's point of view. The line comes from the progress speech that is delivered by the fallen Absalom (ll. 698–722). Before the speech begins, the narrator points to Absalom's deceitful gestures and serpentine manner: "Thus, form'd by Nature, furnish'd out with Arts, / He glides unfelt into their secret hearts" (ll. 692–93). And the speech itself shows us Absalom at his most contemptible. He has been seduced by Achitophel and seems, like Eve in *Paradise Lost,* to have learned the arts of rhetoric and deception from his seducer. The ironic aside toward the end of the speech clearly reveals the narrator's attitude toward Absalom: "Take then my tears (with that he wip'd his Eyes)" (l. 717). We are surely not meant to take Absalom's characterization of David as the narrator's atittude toward the king. My reading, however, does not rest on pointing out that Frost used a bad example to argue that the king is, at the opening of the poem, an idle monarch. For the distinction that Dryden makes, through the eyes of the narrator and various characters, between the person and the office of the king is clear; it is, in fact, the very distinction that David makes as he reluctantly moves from mercy to justice in the closing speech of the poem (ll. 941–42).

13. Schilling, *Conservative Myth,* p. 279.

14. The allusion to Adam in these lines has often been recognized; see, e.g., Hoffman's remarks in *Dryden's Imagery,* p. 74.

15. French, "Dryden, Marvell, and Political Poetry," p. 411.

16. As Schilling notes, Dryden's reference to the birth of Charles II in *Astraea Redux* includes a reference to Charles's nativity star, which obviously suggests the bright star seen at Christ's birth. Schilling makes of this connection the following observation: "This augury of a great future helps persuade Absalom that there is no real difference between himself and his father as king, for when Charles I was on his way to St. Paul's to give thanks for the birth of the future Charles II in 1630, a bright star shone in the sky at mid-day, as already seen in *Astraea Redux,* 288–91" (*Conservative Myth,* p. 268). Yet, if we grant *Absalom and Achitophel* some fictional integrity, we can hardly expect the biblical character Absalom to be impressed with the similarity of his own nativity star to that of Charles II.

17. The relationship between *Absalom and Achitophel* and Milton's epics has been the subject of numerous discussions, the most recent and fullest being Ferry's *Milton and the Miltonic Dryden.*

18. *Samson Agonistes,* ll. 33–34, 68–69.

19. Lewalski, "Scope and Function," pp. 34–35.

20. In *The Sermons of Master Henry Smith, gathered into one volume* (London, 1607), sig. V4v, Smith links the seduction of Eve by Satan to the seduction of Absalom by Achitophel: "As there be two spirites, so there be two doctrines, two wisdomes, and two counsels. In

I. Timoth. 4.1. there is a doctrine of divels: if you heare that doctrine, you hearken to the divell, as *Saul* did to a Witch. In the fifteenth of *Mathew* there is a doctrine of men, which Christ called *Leaven*: if you hearken to that you shall erre like men, because the blinde leade the blinde. In Genesis 3. there is a Counsell of the Serpent: if you hearken to that you shall perish like *Eve*. In the 2. Samuel 18, there is a wisedome of *Achitophel*: if you hearken to that, you shall speede like *Absalon*."

21. Yvor Winters's remarks in *Forms of Discovery* (Denver, 1967), p. 126, represent the opposite critical point of view: "The directly satiric and didactic are not invariably combined with each other, but we find them together in the most memorable poems. I will take *Absalom and Achitophel* and the *Epistle to Arbuthnot* as examples. Most readers— myself among them—remember these poems fragmentarily: the portraits of Zimri, Achitophel, and Atticus, and a handful of Pope's epigrams stay in the mind, but the poems do not. The reason for this is simple: neither poem has any really unifying principle. Dryden employs a dull narrative, which elaborately and clumsily parallels the biblical narrative, and he does this in order to praise a monarch who was a corrupt fool. One cannot take the whole poem seriously, but one can find interest in the brilliant details."

22. *Paradise Lost* 3. 455–58.

23. Lewalski, "Scope and Function," p. 34.

24. Taylor, in *Moses and Aaron*, sigs. E5–E5v, declares, "*David* had his thirty seaven Worthies, that Valiantly fought his battels. . . . So had the Sonne of *David* his twelve Apostles, and seventy two disciples, who . . . fought the Lords spirituall battells, and mightily subdued the world under the government of Jesus Christ."

25. See, e.g., Schilling, *Conservative Myth*, p. 284.

CHAPTER 5

1. Dryden's conversion to Catholicism was, for more than two centuries, a prime target of criticism among his detractors. The conversion itself and Dryden's defense, *The Hind and the Panther* (1687), were attacked and ridiculed in contemporary works like *The Hind and the Panther, Transvers'd* (1687), *The Reasons of Mr. Bays Changing his Religion* (1688), *The Late Converts Exposed: Or The Reasons of Mr. Bays's Changing his Religion* (1690). Hugh Macdonald's *John Dryden: A Bibliography of Early Editions and of Drydeniana* (Oxford, 1939) contains an annotated bibliography of the late seventeenth- and early eighteenth-century attacks on Dryden. Macaulay, in the nineteenth century, mounted a classic attack on Dryden's character. Of Dryden's conversion Macaulay wrote: "Dryden was poor and impatient of poverty. He knew little and cared little about religion. If any sentiment was deeply fixed in him, that sentiment was an aversion to priests of all persuasions. . . . He had, during many years, earned his daily bread by pandaring to the vicious taste of the pit, and by grossly flattering rich

and noble patrons. Self-respect and a fine sense of the becoming were not to be expected from one who had led a life of mendicancy and adulation. Finding that, if he continued to call himself a Protestant, his services would be overlooked, he declared himself a Papist. The King's parsimony speedily relaxed. Dryden's pension was restored: the arrears were paid up; and he was employed to defend his new religion both in prose and verse" (*The History of England*, ed. C. H. Firth, 6 vols. [London, 1913–15], 2:850–52). James Osborn, in *John Dryden: Some Biographical Facts and Problems*, rev. ed. (Gainesville, 1965), pt. 1, writes on the vicissitudes of Dryden's personal reputation.

2. Earl Miner and Phillip Harth have written thorough studies of Dryden's religious beliefs and religious poems. See Miner, *Dryden's Poetry* (Bloomington, Ind., 1967), chap. 5; Miner's introduction and notes to *The Hind and the Panther* in *The Works of John Dryden*, ed. E. N. Hooker and H. T. Swedenberg, Jr. (Berkeley and Los Angeles, 1956–), 3:326–459; and Harth's *Contexts of Dryden's Thought* (Chicago, 1968). Of the possible connections between the political and the religious views in Dryden's poetry of the late 1680s, Harth writes: "The temptation to seek clues to Dryden's religion in his politics is understandable. In the first place, while his religious beliefs changed, his political convictions did not. . . . Secondly, politics was a subject on which Dryden continued to write during the interval between *Religio Laici* and his conversion to the Catholic faith. . . . The biographer, ready to grasp at any straw in frustration, may turn to these works in the hope of finding some clue to the imminent change in Dryden's religion. He will find plentiful references to the political consequences of Catholicism and Dissent of the kind already offered in *Absalom and Achitophel*, *The Medal*, and the latter part of the preface to *Religio Laici*. But he will find no hint of the change of faith that was taking place in the poet's mind and heart. On that matter of crucial importance he remained deliberately silent" (pp. 229–30). My subject is not biography, but I believe that neither Harth nor other students of Dryden's religious thought have considered the relationship between the political poetry and the religious conversion in the manner that I suggest. Although Dryden's politics did not change, Harth's assertion that "his political convictions" remained constant is open to debate. Dryden's belief in political redemption—particularly in the power of the Stuart monarchy to redeem a recalcitrant England—underwent a steady decline between the time of the Exclusion Crisis and the accession of William and Mary. The poet remained silent on the subject of his conversion, but his changing use of scriptural metaphor in his political poetry of the period supplies, I believe, numerous hints of his change of mind and heart. Sanford Budick's *Dryden and the Abyss of Light: A Study of "Religio Laici" and "The Hind and the Panther"* (New Haven, 1970) was published after the present text had been completed.

3. See the discussion in chap. 3 of the king as *typus Christi*. Miner's discussion of *Threnodia Augustalis* (*Works* 3:299–305) analyzes Dryden's handling of the medieval concept of the king's two bodies, referring the reader to Ernst Kantorowicz's *The King's Two Bodies* (Princeton, 1957).

4. I quote, of course, Dryden's translation of the *Aeneid* 6. 786, 788–89. The lines on Salmoneus read:

> *Salmoneus,* suff'ring cruel Pains, I found,
> For emulating *Jove;* the ratling Sound
> Of Mimick Thunder, and the glitt'ring Blaze
> Of pointed Lightnings, and their forky Rays.
> Through *Elis,* and the *Grecian* Towns he flew:
> Th' audacious Wretch four fiery Coursers drew:
> He wav'd a Torch aloft, and, madly vain,
> Sought Godlike Worship from a Servile Train.
>
> .   .   .   .
>
> But he, the King of Heav'n, obscure on high,
> Bar'd his red Arm, and launching from the Sky
> His writhen Bolt, not shaking empty Smoak,
> Down to the deep Abyss the flaming Felon strook.
>
> [6. 788–803]

These lines seem to be directly indebted to Milton's handling of Satan at the opening of *Paradise Lost.* Alan Roper's discussion of *The Medall* in *Dryden's Poetic Kingdoms* (London, 1965) has a number of interesting observations on Dryden's use of *Paradise Lost* in that poem.

5. Without insisting that, for instance, the three spiritual senses of Dante's reading of the biblical episode were preserved by seventeenth-century commentary, one can assume that the composite spiritual significance of Exodus was alive in Dryden's age. See, e.g., the commentary on 2 Peter 2:1 in Joseph Mede's *Works* (London, 1664), sig. Ee6v: "*I am the Lord thy God which brought thee out of the land of Egypt, Thou shalt have none other Gods but me:* In the New Testament thus saith Christ, *I am Christ the Lord which bought thee, Thou shalt have no other Christs but me.* Are not these alike? So when the *Israelites* fell to *Idolatry,* and to worship Idols and strange Gods, hear how the Lord speaks then, *Deut.* 32. 15, 16. *Jeshurun waxed fat, forsook God which made him, and lightly esteemed the Rock of his Salvation; they provoked him to jealousie with strange gods.* So may we say, the Christian Mother *waxed fat, forsook God which redeemed her, &c.* Judges 2. 12, 13. *They forsook the Lord God of their Fathers, which brought them out of the land of Egypt, and followed other gods, and served Baal and Ashtaroth.* And this expression is frequent, *Psal.* 81. 10, 11. I *King.* 9. 9. 2 *King.* 17. 7. Just so might the Lord speak of Christians; *They forsook the Lord which brought them out of the Spirituall Egypt,* and worshipped *Saints* and *Angels.*" In 1660 Milton concluded *The Ready and Easy Way* by invoking the same scriptural image with the same moral implications, though, of course, with a political intent opposite to that of Dryden: "But I trust I shall have spoken perswasion to abundance of sensible and ingenuous men: to som perhaps whom God may raise of these stones to become children of reviving libertie; and may reclaim, though they seem now chusing them a captain back for *Egypt,* to bethink themselves a little and consider whether they are rushing" (*The Works of John Milton,* ed. Frank A. Patterson, 18 vols. [New York, 1931–38], vol. 6, ed. Patterson, William Haller, and George Philip Krapp [1932], pp. 148–49). Thomas Pierce, in an

anniversary sermon on the king's restoration, invokes the theme of
Egyptian bondage from the same political perspective as Dryden.
Preaching on a text from Deuteronomy 6:12, "Then beware lest thou
forget the Lord, which brought thee forth out of the land of Egypt,"
Pierce applies the particulars of the biblical text to the present day:
"First behold the *greatest Curse* that any poor Nation can struggle
under. A *yoke* of *Bondage* and *Captivity*, impos'd by the *hardest* and
worst of men. A *yoke* so insupportable to some mens *Necks,* that I
remember *Hegesistratus* (a captive Souldier in *Herodotus*) would rather
cut off his *legs,* than *indure* his *Fetters;* that by the *loss* of his *Feet,* he
might be enabled to *run away.* So insufferable a thing is the *state* of
Thraldome, very significantly imply'd in the *Land of Egypt,* and
exegetically express'd by *the House of Bondage*" (*A Sermon preached
. . . before the . . . House of Commons . . . upon the anniversary day
of the King's and Kingdomes restauration* [London, 1661], sig. B3).

6. John Riland's Restoration sermon *Elias the Second, his Coming
to Restore All Things: or Gods way of Reforming by Restoring* (Oxford,
1662), sigs. H2v–H3, captures something of the angry, impatient mood
of *The Medall:* "Many thousands we know came short of *Canaan,*
meerly for their *murmuring* and *mis-believing;* And we, if we still
joyn with those *Jewes* in their repining notes, *Wherefore came we forth
of Egypt, here's neither bread nor water. Our soul loaths this light
bread.* If so, then as we *partake* with them in their *Sins,* let's beware we
share not with them in their *Sufferings,* and so the Lord send *Serpents*
amongst *us,* even as he did amongst *them.* A *sly* and subtile generation,
that are *wise* as *Serpents,* but *innocent* as *Eagles* or *Vultures,* and long
to be dividing the *Prey* upon the *Carcases* of the *two grand
Combatants.*"

7. Dryden was not the only Royalist to apply the parable to the
political events that culminated in the Exclusion Crisis. Nicholas Adee
preached his *Plot for a Crown, in a visitation-sermon at Cricklade, May
the fifteenth 1682* (London, 1685) on Luke 20:14. James Kinsley places
the publication of *The Medall* on or just before 16 March 1682 (*The
Poems of John Dryden,* 4 vols. [Oxford, 1958], 4:1906).

8. See, e.g., John Richardson, *Choice Observations and Explanations
upon the Old Testament* (London, 1655), sigs. P2v–P3.

9. Alexander Ross, in his commentary on Hercules in *Mystagogus
Poeticus,* 6th ed. (London, 1675), sig. M5, links the verse from
Revelation to the classical myth: "Our blessed Saviour is the true
Hercules, who was the true and only Son of God, & of the Virgin *Mary:*
who was persecuted out of malice, and exposed to all dangers, which
he overcame: he subdued the roaring Lion, that red Dragon, that tyrant
and devourer of mankind, the devil."

10. Cf. William Guild's interpretation of David's altar sacrifice in
The Throne of David (Oxford, 1658), sig. Xx1v: "This Alter must be
reared up, in the threshing floore of *Arannah* the *Jebusite,* which was
(as we have shewne) upon Mount *Moriah,* so that on that very hill, where
the Angell held the sword of *Abraham,* from killing his sonne *Isaac,*
who was a tipe of Christ: doth God now with hold the sword of the

Angell, from killing his people, and upon this very ground after, did the temple also stand, where the holy Altar should be, whereon the expiatory, and propitiatory, sacrifices for Gods people, should be offered up in succeeding generations, not without a mysterie of that oblation of Christ Jesus (as is said) prefigured by *Isaac,* and whose blessed body, was the True Temple, tiped by that of *Solomon,* as Christ himselfe shewes, *Joh.* 2. 19. And his oblation of himselfe, is that expiatory, and propitiatory sacrifice, by which Gods wrath is appeased, and we reconciled unto God his Father."

CONCLUSION

1. *Restoration Comedy, 1660–1720* (London, 1924), p. 104.

INDEX